Germinal G. Van

ESSAYS ON ISSUES

The Fundamentals Of American Politics

(Volume 1)

Copyright©2019 by Germinal G. Van
All Rights Reserved
Book written by Germinal G. Van
and edited by John Jaros
Cover designed by Germinal G. Van
Published by Germinal G. Van and Kindle Direct Publishing
authorgerminalgvan@gmail.com
ISBN: 978-1717817945
Printed in the United States

ESSAYS ON ISSUES

The Fundamentals Of American Politics

(Volume 1)

Table of Contents

The Author

Germinal G. Van is an author, political essayist, an independent scholar, and a member of the Midwest Political Science Association (MPSA) who focuses his work on political theory, constitutional politics, political economy and social theory. He was born in 1990 and raised in Abidjan, Côte d'Ivoire. He moved to the United States in 2010.

He graduated from the Catholic University of America in 2014 with a B.A. in Political Science and obtained an M.A. in Political Management from the George Washington University in 2017.

Germinal published his first book in April 2018. The book is entitled *American Political Culture: An Observation from The Outside.* He published a second book within the same year. The second book is entitled *Equal Under The Law: A*

Reflection on Amendment XIV and the Concept of Citizenship. Essay On Issues is his third published work.

Acknowledgements

I would like to, first and foremost, thank my wife and my sister for their contribution to the realization of this manuscript.

I would, secondly, want to thank Professor Keita for his loyal contribution my work. Mr. Mohamed Balla Keita is a Professor of Political Science at the George Washington University. He holds a Ph.D. from Howard University.

Thirdly, I want to thank John Jaros for his extensive editorial work on the manuscript. John Jaros, holds a Bachelor's degree in History from DePaul University.

Finally, I would like to thank my dear friend, John P. Fahy, a former Member of the Board of Education of Warren Township, New Jersey, for his intellectual contribution for the realization of this book. John and I attended the Catholic University of America. He holds a Bachelor's degree in Biochemistry since 2012.

Preface

Essays On Issues: The Fundamentals Of American Politics is a two-volume book that focuses on the current political issues in America. It primarily encapsulates my political philosophy on the major issues such as national defense, foreign policy, education, immigration...etc. I believe that it is important that an individual living in a civil society ought to have a shape of political thoughts about any single issue that we are facing as a collectivity. Politics is involved in our daily lives, whether we like it or not, whether we are interested in it or not. Every day, a group of individuals passes and implements laws that affect our lives positively and negatively. It also affects our lives individually and collectively. As I have been living in the most powerful nation in the world for nine years now, and as a permanent resident, I am more than ever incorporated into the American culture and the American way of life. It entails that, whatever law, policy or regulation that the government implements, it affects me directly since I have subjected myself to the laws and authority of the United States government, and therefore, to the subsequent jurisdiction I reside in.

By writing this book, I decided to take a deep approach onward the major issues that are part of the daily life of the ordinary American citizen. Throughout this reading, you, the reader, will formulate your own views about my political philosophy. One sure thing I can say to you is that I am a staunch advocate of a republican government. By using the word republican, I do not imply at all the Republican Party—I do imply the doctrines of representative democracy as James Madison envisioned for this country. I am an uncompromising believer of the United States

Constitution, an avid supporter of the rule of law, due process, and the separation of powers. Overall, I am a defender of liberty, individual freedom, and equality under the law for all individuals living in the United States of America. Some will surely disagree with my views. Nevertheless, my political views are purely and genuinely based upon constitutional principles. I do not take stance based on the leisure of playing party politics. I do not believe in it because it is divisive. I do take stance for issues that I believe are fundamentally constitutional, and constitutionally principled. I do stand for the preservation of the constitutional order, which is the bedrock of the American political culture. If we do not do our best to preserve, protect and defend the constitutional order, we will be jeopardizing and compromising our democracy, and the foundations of our constitutional republic.

As I previously stated, the manuscript is made into two volumes. The first volume is divided into four main essays. Each essay is also composed of five sub-essays that elaborate upon various aspects of each issue, except the third essay which treats of the issue of immigration law, and thereby composed of four sub-essays. The first essay highlights the fundamentals of American liberal democracy. It articulates on the notion of popular sovereignty, individual liberties, the role of the government, state's rights and the electoral college. The second essay dissects the issue of foreign policy and national security. It discusses upon the concept of American foreign policy, the issue of expansionism, the problem of military spending, the question of foreign spending, and of the NATO and the United Nations. The third essay responds upon the issue of immigration law. It delivers an analysis upon the reasons of why DACA should be preserved or dissolved, explains the great costs of having the border wall, epitomizes upon the essence of the Diversity Visa Program and articulates on the problematic question of the Immigration and Customs Enforcement (ICE). The fourth and last essay encompasses the basic issues of education policy. The debate on education policy encloses five sub-essays. An essay that establishes my view upon the privatization of education; the second essay epitomizes my philosophy regarding Common Core. The third sub-essay is devoted to school prayers, the fourth on school vouchers and the fifth on vocational school. I have, nonetheless, added a last essay to the book as an supplementary issue that needed to be addressed. The essay principally concentrates on the issue of secularism in the United States.

The very purpose of disclosing my political philosophy is for the reader to understand the essence of my thoughts, and the grounds upon which I constructed my views on every issue. At the end of the readings, some of you may or will assert that I am conservative, or that I am against progressivism. I am not against progressivism nor that I am conservative. Yet, I do believe that constant and rapid changes impede society's progress—it destabilizes the status-quo. When a political order is implemented for the sake of taking society into a specific direction, it is important that, that society experiments the motion of that political order—to accustom itself to it and make of it a new tradition; because society relies upon tradition and precedent. That is why, throughout my writings, you will see that I am philosophically more or less oriented to the right of the political exchequer. The views that I offer are strictly mine. They are only the reflection of my political philosophy on political issues. In the second volume, I intended to expand on broader issues such as the economy, law and order, social issues, and my legal philosophy.

Germinal G. Van

Part I

On The Fundamentals of American Democracy

I.

On Popular Sovereignty

The most fundamental notion that establishes the pillars of American democracy is the concept of popular sovereignty. Popular sovereignty stands for *rule by the people.* It is a political doctrine that is rooted in the principle that the authority of a state and its government is created and sustained by the consent of the people[1]. It signifies that the will of the people is represented through their elected representatives.

The popular sovereignty entrenches the concept of self-government and participatory democracy. Thomas Jefferson, who was the third President of the United States and the father of the Declaration of Independence, envisioned a constitution that would prevail popular sovereignty. He [Thomas Jefferson] insisted that the purpose of the Constitution of the United States is to empower the citizen and to constrain the power of the federal government. As the principal goal of popular sovereignty is to let the people decide for themselves, it thus, commences at the utmost

---

[1] Wikipedia Contributors, " Popular Sovereignty".
Wikipedia, The Free Encyclopedia, August 6, 2018. Web.

smallest size of government, which means local government.

As Thomas Jefferson was, I am a staunch advocate of decision-making at the local government level. It is within local politics that participatory democracy is the most effective. Participatory democracy is the most efficient at the local level of the political realm because the people that constitute the popular sovereignty of that political realm are directly involved in the decision-making of that political space. Like in Ancient Greece with the city-state of Athens wherein direct democracy was best reflected and represented, participatory democracy is the synonym of Athenian democracy in America. Participatory democracy works best in a smaller geographical area like in a town, city, or in a county. These geographical realms enumerated are where local government is the highest form of political authority.

A direct democracy is a system in which the people ascertain their sovereignty by directly voting on the matter, instead of approaching the issue through the mediation of an elected representative. Popular sovereignty is not only reflected at the smallest scale of government in a political realm. On a wider scale, popular sovereignty is emulated in a representative democracy or indirect democracy. It entails that the will of the people is delineated in the legislature, through an elected representative. Undoubtedly, it is quasi-impossible for a strict participatory democracy to truly work at a wider scale or larger level of government such state government or the federal government. Furthermore, we must not forget that the United States is a federation. In a federation, only representative democracy can truly promulgate popular sovereignty on a national scale. Popular sovereignty was also included in Article V of the United States Constitution, which provides the means to amend the Constitution through elected representatives of the people[2].

---

[2] Patrick, John, "Popular Sovereignty", *Understanding Democracy*, Annenberg Classroom. www.annenbergclassroom.org. Article. Web.

Regardless of how the nation-state gains power, its citizens are usually given certain rights[3]. As a result, the nation-state has certain rights such as liberty, freedom from outside forces—this freedom is called popular sovereignty[4]. The concept of popular sovereignty essentially says that the collective identity of a nation-state's people possesses the right to liberty from oppression by outside sources[5]. The legitimacy of popular sovereignty is determined in the precept of accountability, which refers to the fact of holding government officials responsible before the law. In *Democracy In America,* Alexis de Tocqueville warned us about the overpower of the legislature. De Tocqueville feared that if the legislature is too mighty, it could arbitrarily encroach the rights of the citizens, consequently undermines popular sovereignty.

---

[3] Khan, Aliya, "Popular Sovereignty", *Learning To Give,* www.learningtogive.org. Article. Web.
[4] Ibid.
[5] Ibid.

Sovereignty is the ultimate source of political power or political authority within a realm[6]. An ultimate authority is the highest element of a continuous chain of direct governance[7]. This ultimate authority is entrenched in the people, which allows them to truly decide for themselves. Primarily, throughout the history of western political thought, ultimate power was solely attributed to the monarch—an individual who singularly ruled over the political realm. Popular sovereignty began to take shape during the Enlightenment Era with Locke, Rousseau and Hobbes. In my first book entitled *American Political Culture: An Observation From The Outside*, I asserted that John Locke is indeed, the originator of the conceptualization of popular sovereignty in modern political thought. He believed that a civil society can only function if the power of the people is sovereign. It suggested that government operates

---

[6] Morris, Christopher W. "The Very Idea of Popular Sovereignty: We The People Reconsidered", *Department of Philosophy, Bowling Green State University* (2000). Article.

[7] Ibid.

from the consent of the popular will, and not as if it was its own mere will. Nonetheless, it is essential to comprehend that the power of American popular sovereignty is grounded in the supremacy of the rule of law.

Maintaining the rule of law indicates that the government is not above the people, but works for the people. Popular sovereignty must be actuated in the sovereignty of the law. The people have delegated power, a limited political power to the government in various capacities. Whenever a government entity transgresses the limits of its delegation by acting ultra vires, it ceases to act in the name of the sovereign[8], and surrenders any derivative sovereign immunity it might otherwise possess[9]. As John Locke enunciated in his book *Second Treatise of Government*, political authority shall be vested in the citizen in order to concise the power of the government. That is why the citizen must initially give his consent to government—

---

[8] Amar, Akhil Reed, "Of Sovereignty and Federalism". *Yale Law School legal Scholarship Repository.* (1987). Article. Paper 1021.
[9] Ibid.

because once the citizen gives his consent to the government, he subsequently legitimizes the political authority that he is vesting into government. It additionally implies that the citizen has delegated some of his power to the government without surrendering the entirety of his rights. The citizen abides to be governed in exchange for the government to protect his rights. It is in this perspective that the power of popular sovereignty is absolute. I must say that the greatest component of the doctrine of popular sovereignty is to hold the government accountable before the law. A civil society that has the capability to hold its government accountable before the law is on that account, empowered to be call "sovereign" because it enshrines the democratic process.

II.

On Individual Liberties

A civil society cannot be wholly democratic if its citizens are not free. Free in the context that the citizen is entitled to political liberties that he freely exercises within the political realm. Individual liberties are the cornerstone of the power of the citizen, the power of an individual living in a politically organized society. Individual liberties derive from the precept of natural rights. The foundations of natural rights took place in the Declaration of Independence. The conceptualization of natural rights in America departed from the point that "all men are created equal". This famous phrase, however, did not originate from Thomas Jefferson. He [Thomas Jefferson] used his theory of natural rights from John Locke to justify the reasons why the American colonies shall secede from the United Kingdom. Locke wrote that all individuals are equal in the sense that they are born with certain inalienable rights[10]. That is, rights that are given by God and can never be taken or given away[11].

These foundational rights are encapsulated in the right to life, which means that an individual shall not be deprived of his life by another individual or by the government; in the right to liberty, which suggests that an individual is free to express his satisfaction and disenchantment to the government without fear of repercussions; and in the right to property, which insinuates that an individual living in a politically organized society is entitled to ownership and private property. Locke believed that the most basic human law is the preservation of mankind[12]. To serve that purpose, he reasoned that individuals have both rights and a duty to preserve their own lives[13]. Furthermore, Locke maintained that individuals should be free to make choices about how to conduct their own lives

---

[10] "The Declaration of Independence and Natural Rights", *Constitutional Rights Foundation.* www.crf-usa.org. Article. Web.
[11] Ibid.
[12] Ibid.
[13] Ibid.

as long as they do not interfere with the liberty of others[14]. The political philosophy of Locke on natural rights determined the principles of individual liberties in the Declaration of Independence that Thomas Jefferson pronounced on July 4, 1776. Natural rights are what entrenched the individual liberties of the American citizen. Interestingly, natural rights are the legal rights that bound the citizen. It guarantees equal treatment and protection of all individuals before the law.

I deeply believe in natural rights because they are the roots of our democracy, the roots of our freedom, and the root of our sovereignty. Political philosophers like Samuel Adams or Thomas Paine made the natural rights theory a powerful justification for revolution[15]. The classic expressions of natural rights are the English Bill of Rights (1689), the American Declaration of Independence (1776), the French Declaration of the Rights of Man and the Citizen (1789), the first ten

---

[14] Ibid.
[15] "natural rights" *The Columbia Electronic Encyclopedia* (1994).

amendments to the Constitution of the United States (1791), and the Universal Declaration of Human Rights of the United Nations (1948)[16]. As we can perceive in the United States Constitution, the citizen is empowered to rebel against his government if he believes that the government has failed to protect his rights and liberties. This principle is enumerated in the Bill of Rights to the United States Constitution.

The Bill of Rights provides to the citizen of the United States, a certain amount of political liberties that significantly restrain the power of the government over the individual. Among the ten amendments that ascertain the sovereignty of the citizen, there are precisely four amendments that legitimize the power of the citizen—the First Amendment, the Third Amendment, the Fourth Amendment, and the Ninth Amendment.

The First Amendment to the Constitution of the United States is the very fundamental right of the citizen in American civil society. It undeniably

---

[16] Ibid.

articulates the first freedom and the nature of that freedom[17]. It guarantees the freedom essential to humans as rational being[18]. The First Amendment epitomizes the freedom of expression and the freedom of religion. These two elements of civil liberty characterize the role of the citizen in democratic civil society. Our most basic beliefs answer the most basic questions that can logically be asked[19]. These include beliefs about authority, existence and value.[20]The essence of the First Amendment is the right of all to their own interpretation of religion, not just the right to their conviction[21]. It encapsulates the precept that the government cannot impose a particular religion upon the citizen. The United States is a democratic

---

[17] Anderson, Owen, "Why the First Amendment is 'First in importance'", *The Washington Times,* (2016). www.washingtontimes.com. Article. Web.
[18] Ibid.
[19] Ibid.
[20] Ibid.
[21] Reisner, Avram Israel, "The First Amendment Protects Religious Freedom, But Also Freedom From Religion". *The Baltimore Sun.* (2012). www.articles.baltimoresun.com. Article. Web.

society where we each have free speech.[22] Our own opinions do not preclude others from having different or contradictory views[23]. The freedom of expression gives the right to assemble and the right denounce as the right to blaspheme. Overall, the First Amendment establishes the core freedom of the citizen in American civil society.

The Third Amendment is not very common to the average American citizen. Nevertheless, it instigates a quintessential role in individual liberties. The Third Amendment stresses the right to domestic privacy. It was designed to protect the citizen against government's intrusion. It signifies that, unless the government has the legal authority to intrude itself in the citizen's private life for whatever reasons or circumstances, it cannot deprive the citizen of liberty without legitimate justification. The Third Amendment is the only part of the Constitution that deals directly with the relationship between the rights of individuals and

---

[22] Editorial Board, "Our Bedrock, the First Amendment" *Democrat & Chronicle* (2016). www.democratandchronicle.com. Article. Web.
[23] Ibid.

the military in both peace and wars[24]. It emphasizes upon the importance of civilian control over the armed forces[25].

The Fourth Amendment accentuates on unreasonable and unfair search and seizure from the government. The Fourth Amendment is basically the sequel of the third. It clearly protects the citizen against an arbitrary action of the government that could lead to unlawful deprivation of property. It yields the inalienable right of the citizen to preserve, protect and defend what rightfully belongs to him. Beforehand, we must fathom what search and seizure are. In the 1886 Supreme Court Case *Boyd v. United States*, Justice Joseph P. Bradley, delivering the opinion of the Court, struck down the customs statute and in doing so, widened the scope of the Fourth Amendment[26]. He argued, "It is not the breaking of a man's doors and the rummaging of his

---

[24] Wood, Gordon S., "The Third Amendment" *Common Interpretation.* www.constitutioncenter.org. Article, Web.
[25] Ibid.
[26] Leming, Robert S. "Teaching about the Fourth Amendment's Protection against Unreasonable Searches and Seizures". *ERIC Clearinghouse for Social Studies.* (1993). Article.

drawers that constitutes the essence of the offense; but it is the invasion of his indefeasible right of personal security, personal liberty, and private property, where that right has never been forfeited by his conviction of some public offense."[27]

The Ninth Amendment is the completion of others rights not enumerated in the United States Constitution. The purpose of the Ninth Amendment was to ensure that all individual natural rights had the same stature and force after some of them were enumerated as they had before; and its existence argued against a latitudinarian interpretation of federal powers[28]. The principal challenge is to identify a conceptual model that best fits the interpretation of the Ninth Amendment[29]. According to the individual rights model, the Ninth Amendment was meant to preserve the other individual, natural, preexisting rights that were retained by the people when forming a government

---

[27] Ibid.
[28] Barnett, Randy E. " The Ninth Amendment: It Means What It Says" *Faculty Scholarship Georgetown University Law Center.* (2006). Article.
[29] Ibid.

but were not included in the "enumeration of certain rights"[30]. In other words, the purpose of the Ninth Amendment was to ensure the equal protection of unenumerated individual natural rights on a par with those individual natural rights that came to be listed for "greater caution" in the Bill of Rights[31]. The greatness of American democracy is grounded in the individual liberties of the citizen. It is the chief element that keeps government's power in checks and obliviates tyranny before the establishment of separation of powers.

---

[30] Ibid.
[31] Ibid.

III.

On The Role of The Government

No matter the level of industrialization of a given nation, its society is considered civil from the moment there is a government. The purpose of government is to regulate society, to protect its citizens and to administer economic development through the implementation of infrastructures. We all agree upon the basic precepts of government. However, the substantial question about government is to know to what extent it intervenes in citizen's life. Is government the solution to our economic and social issues? These questions were raised at the genesis of American politics.

The role of government has been the object of philosophical disagreement between the Jeffersonians (supporters of the political philosophy of Thomas Jefferson) and the Hamiltonians (supporters of the political philosophy of Alexander Hamilton). For the Jeffersonians, government, when it moved beyond the elementary obligations of police and defense, served only to transfer wealth from producers in farm and field to the financial aristocracy[32]. The Jeffersonians concluded, therefore, that that government was best which governed least[33]. For the Hamiltonians, on the other hand, the national government was precisely the means by which to transform a static pastoral society into a booming industrial nation[34]. Hamilton believed in the dynamics of individual acquisition , but only if tempered by a measure of public control[35]. The complete antagonism between the two political philosophies substantiated the significance of the role of government.

From where I was born, the government has played an active in the citizen's life and continues to do so. The major reasons for such government's encroachment is primarily based upon the fact that the Republic of Côte d'Ivoire is a country of twenty-

---

[32] Utley Jr., Robert L., The Tocqueville Forum, "The Idea of Affirmative Government in American History", *The Promise of American Politics: Principles and Practices After Two Hundred Years.* University Press of America, Inc. (1989). P.17. Print.
[33] Ibid. P.17.
[34] Ibid. P.17.
[35] Ibid. P.18

five million inhabitants, which gives the ability to the government to easily manage the people. Secondarily, political power is concentrated in the executive branch. The problem with centralized government like the one in Côte d'Ivoire, France, Italy, China and many unitary systems, is that that kind of political regime has a very strong executive, which automatically leads to the tyranny of the government because it arbitrarily subjugates the rights of the citizens to a condition. This condition obliviates the citizen from any form of emancipation (political, economic, or social) because it constrains him to only fit certain criteria predetermined by the government. Whereas the principle of natural rights allows the citizen to entitlement and the right to possess without necessary government's consent. In the United States, therewith three hundred million inhabitants, it is surely burdensome to centralize power in the national government. I am therefore in favor of a limited government rather than an expanded one. Although government is a societal necessity; I, nonetheless, do not believe that it is the cure or the remedy to citizenry's issues.

What I believe is that government ought to be limited to the smallest possible scope. The national government shall only intervene when local or state governments fail to respond to the citizens' needs. Other than that specific condition, societal issues shall be solved by local authorities. Limited government is quintessential because it fosters individual liberties and promulgates economic growth. It is important to comprehend that advocates of limited government are not anti-government, they are hostile to concentration of coercive power and to the arbitrary use of power against rights[36]. Whether, James Madison was a proponent of national government, he, nevertheless, discerned the fears of his fellow countrymen upon a potential tyrannical power of the national government. He subsequently, in *The Federalist Paper No 45*, elaborated upon the "enumerated

---

[36] Palmer, Tom G., "2. Limited Government and the Rule of Law" *Cato Handbook For Policymakers, 8th Edition.* (2017) www.cato.org. Article.

powers" that define the scope of the national government by the United States Constitution. The principle of limited government expands upon the idea of popular sovereignty[37]. The Constitution is the place where we state, clearly and explicitly, which powers we choose to give to the government and which powers we refuse to give to it.[38]

I am adamantly convinced that a limited government is more suitable for a democratic and prosperous society than an embellished one. Limited government is less expensive because it limits the amount of governmental agencies. We must not forget that ultimately, we are the taxpayers, which means that the financial contribution for the creation of these governmental programs and agencies are deducted from our paychecks. A smaller government cuts down on waste, fraud and inefficiency[39]. It is in fact difficult

---

[37] Shmoop Editorial Team., "Limited Government", Shmoop University Inc. November 11, 2008, www.shmoop.com/constitution/limited-government.
[38] Ibid.
[39] Penna, Sue Ann, "The Benefits of a Limited Government", *Bloomfield Patch.* (2012). www.patch.com . Article, Web.

46

to keep track of the government's activities when it contains numerous governmental programs. It allows to regulate the level of accountability of the government's action and of government's officials. Limited government values individual and economic freedom[40]. Less government means less intrusion into our lives[41]. It suggests that we can live our lives as we see fit, not how the government sees fit[42]. The individual is left with the responsibility of his or her own decisions and actions[43]. Economically speaking, limited government enlarges the creation of local business over corporation. It gives a chance to any individual to enterprise and create personal business. Limited government empowers the individual and consolidates individualism.

The role of the government is ordained by the principle of separation of powers. The principle of separation of powers ensures that one branch of government does not overuse its power over the two

---

[40] Ibid.
[41] Ibid.
[42] Ibid.
[43] Ibid.

other branches. I personally call for an accentuation on the separation of powers. I propose a strong emphasis on the separation of powers because it checks the power of the national government and safeguards the freedom of the citizens. I do not need to reiterate the basic elements that constitute the concept of separation of powers. My political philosophy on the matter is centralized upon the preponderance that the separation of powers plays in the life of the citizen. As we are living in a representative democracy, the federal and state legislatures are the reflection of the popular will. It [the legislature] supervises the implementation of the laws and policies exhilarated by the executive branch. Albeit, the legislative body is the legitimate representation of popular sovereignty; it, yet, can abuse its power in certain conditions or circumstances. That is why the judiciary is compelling and essential for the good functioning of government. It secures the integrity of the public opinion and upholds the precepts of self-government that are entrenched in the Constitution. The principle of the separation of powers punctuates the substance of the rule of law. It authenticates the rule of majority. It is imperative to reaffirm its authority in order to preserve the supremacy of the rule of law.

IV.

On State's Rights

This essay may seem controversial to some people. But I think, through an accurate reading, the reader will fathom my stances upon the matter of state's rights. Indeed, I support state's rights whether many people would find it odd and contentious. Most African Americans hold the concept of state's rights in contempt because it enhanced slavery in southern states—and I do totally understand that. However, I am an advocate of state's rights for two distinguished reasons.

The primary reason for my intellectual support in favor of state's rights is grounded upon the concept of political decentralization. I have reiterated numerous times that true sovereignty is invigorated when political power is decentralized. The decentralization of political power from the central government ensures the preservation of the sovereignty of local and state governments. The second reason for my support in favor of state's rights is entrenched in the right to self-determination. I have always supported the Anti-Federalist philosophy on state's rights because they championed states' sovereignty and states' rights protect individual liberties and the right to self-determination. Included in the Bill of Rights that was adopted, was also the Tenth Amendment, which reserved all unallocated rights to the states and to the people[44]. As a matter of fact, the Tenth Amendment to the United States Constitution established the limpid separation between the power of the federal government and state government. It consolidates the legitimacy of state's authority and substantiates the right to self-determination of the people.

The argument of states' rights began even before the drafting of the Constitution[45]. The Articles of Confederation created in it a strong respect for states' rights and left a very weak federal government[46]. Many proponents of states' rights felt that state's rights should be afforded greater weight and in that regard the Tenth Amendment was

---

[44] "State's Right" www.u-s-history.com

[45] "States' Rights" www.constitution.laws.com
[46] Ibid.

drafted to appease those individuals concerned with centralized power[47].

I believe that, in order to substantially understand the essence of state's rights, it is essential to fathom the meaning of the Tenth Amendment. The Tenth Amendment declares "*The powers not delegated to the United States by the Constitution, nor prohibited by it to the States, are reserved to the States respectively or to the people*"[48]. It emphasized that the inclusion of a bill of rights does not change the fundamental character of the national government[49]. It remains a government of limited and enumerated powers[50], so that the first question involving an exercise of federal power is not whether it violates someone's rights, but whether it exceeds the national government's enumerated powers[51]. The Tenth Amendment serves as a system of checks and balances by providing a

---

[47] Ibid.
[48] Lawson, Gary, Schapiro, Robert; "The Tenth Amendment" *Common Interpretation.* www.constitutioncenter.org. Article. Web.
[49] Ibid.
[50] Ibid.
[51] Ibid.

certain authority to the states, which would prevent the central government from garnering too much power and creating the potential of what the United States already had experienced with England[52]. Under the Tenth Amendment, each government possesses direct authority over citizens—the states over their citizens and the federal government under its assigned powers[53].

I must admit that, although I support state's rights, certain issues such slavery, women's rights to vote in 1920 through the implementation of the Nineteenth Amendment, the Civil Rights Act of 1964, and the LGBTQ rights—all needed federal government intervention because the essence of human dignity was violated and dehumanized. It was under humiliating circumstances that African Americans had to endure appalling treatments like lynching, and segregation in southern states and in

---

[52]   "Understanding the 10th Amendment". www.constitution.laws.com

[53] Cooper, Charles "The Constitution in One Sentence: Understanding the Tenth Amendment". *The Heritage Foundation.* January 10, 2011, www.heritage.org. Article. Web.

some northern states, until the national government abolished slavery. The right to vote was forbidden to women until the 1920s and was deprived to African Americans until 1965. Both categories were denied citizenship on the basis that women were only meant to reproduce and taking care of babies; and African Americans were meant to be second-class citizens. It was therefore important that the national government intervened in order to uphold the principle that "all men are equal under the law" and the rule of law itself. The same view is also applied to LGBT rights because many United States citizens who serve in our armed forces have been subjected to discrimination based upon their sexual orientation. It is the duty of the national government to protect the rights of these individuals who fight to safeguard our freedom, against all forms of discriminations. Nonetheless, I consider that some issues such marijuana policy, health law, education policy, and abortion rights shall be left to the states. I, for instance, consider that marijuana policy shall be left to the state because it is an issue that needs to not be nationalized. It is an issue that should be solely solved between the people and their legislatures. Criminalizing or legalizing marijuana is purely a matter of state's politics. I believe about that same approach for education, which I will further develop on the matter in the subsequent parts of the book— and for abortion rights and for health policies. My stances on health law will be posteriorly elaborated in the second volume. I do want, nevertheless, to address the issue of abortion rights within this essay.

The choice of a woman to terminate or keep her pregnancy, I believe, solely depends upon her, in my modest opinion. I think that abortion rights should have therefore been left to the states to decide to implement policies that would either legalize or restrict abortion because abortion rights are not initially encapsulated in the scope of the Fourteenth Amendment. There is nothing in the United States Constitution that directly address the issue of pregnancy. Consequently, whereas the US Supreme Court is the highest court in the land, it was not its role to decide upon its [abortion rights] legalization because the relevance of abortion rights derives from the personal liberty of the citizen and its legal rights toward the state. Instead of focusing on the Fourteenth Amendment to determine upon the right of privacy, the Supreme Court should have used the Ninth Amendment to entrench the right of privacy. Indeed, the Ninth Amendment is the amendment that empowers the people not as a collectivity but as an individual to freely choose for himself or herself without any interference and against the power of the government. By failing to use the Ninth Amendment to determine the right of privacy, the Supreme Court of the United States used the wrong amendment, and therefore went beyond the scope of its power which I believe, is to interpret the law, and not to legislate it. When the Court legislates a law, it impedes it impartiality and therefore, undermines the democratic process. Those in favor of abortion rights but living in conservative states for instance, should engage a petition in the state of affairs in order to exercise a significant influence in their legislature for the sake of decriminalizing abortion. But I do not believe that it was the role of the national government, in particular the judiciary, to decide upon the matter, because it is an issue that should have been left between the individual and the state. One way to fight for abortion rights in conservative states is to use the electoral process to oust incumbent legislators who have criminalized abortion. Nonetheless, my disagreement with the Supreme Court's final decision on *Roe v. Wade* does not imply at all that *Roe* should be overturned. Since 1973, abortion has been legalized in the United States and it is a decision that became the law of the land regarding abortion rights. As *Roe* became the law of the land, and subsequently a precedent, It must be upheld. If I were a judge or a Supreme Court Justice, I would have never overturned *Roe v. Wade* because it is a judicial precedent and it does surely protect women to freely exercise their right to choose to keep or terminate their pregnancy. In the second volume of *Essays On Issues*, I will deepen my views on abortion rights because it is a crucial right in American society. I do support abortion rights because I believe it is the woman's fundamental right to choose for herself, but the essence of my disagreement with the Supreme Court's reasoning in determining the case is based on its procedure.

V.

On The Electoral College

The Electoral College system has been despised for two major controversial presidential elections that shaped the course of American politics. The first election that changed the course of history at the dawn of the twenty-first century, was the contentious victory of George W. Bush in 2000. George W. Bush, then-Governor of the State of Texas, lost the popular vote to Al Gore, but won the presidency through the Electoral College. The second election that affected the American political aqueduct, was the controversial White House conquest of Donald J. Trump in 2016. Trump was defeated in the popular vote by Former Secretary of State and U.S. Senator, Hillary Rodham Clinton, nonetheless, won the White House by the wonders of the Electoral College. Many Americans believe that the Electoral College is not anymore suitable to remain the determining factor of a presidential election. Some even adopted a more radical stance by calling for its unmitigated abolition, if necessary, without following the constitutional procedure that leads to its revocation. If the Electoral College was incorporated into the Constitution of the United

States in the first place, it is because the wisdom of the Founding Fathers was greater than the short-termed dissatisfaction of the people.

The Founding Fathers established the Electoral College in the Constitution as a compromise between the election of the President by a vote in Congress and election of the President by a popular vote of qualified citizens[54]. In a presidential election, the popular vote simply means an aggregate of all voters from all states in America[55]. The Electoral College is not necessarily the greatest system to elect a president because, as a component of a political system, it, irrefutably, has its flaws. Nevertheless, I assert that it is the most effective electoral system to elect the President. It is an efficient system of electoral politics because we live in a representative democracy. In a representative democracy built under federalism, the Electoral College best reflects the sovereignty of the states, thenceforward, the

---

[54] "What is the Electoral College?" *National Archives and Records Administration.* www.archives.org Article. Web.
[55] "Electoral Vote vs. Popular Vote" www.diffen.com Article, Web.

popular sovereignty. Notwithstanding the fact that the Electoral College may cerebrates some failures in its functioning, I do not reckon that popular vote is the adequate solution to elect the President of the United States. I, by consequence of that, stand in favor of the sustentation of the Electoral College.

The preservation of the Electoral College protects the rights of smaller states and its cornerstone of American federalism[56]. States can design their own mechanism without federal involvement—for choosing their electors[57]. Undoubtedly, the Electoral College gives a voice to smaller and weaker states. It allows these states to be fairly and satisfactorily represented throughout the electoral process. The Electoral College system stiffened the principles of federalism that the Founding Fathers have envisioned at the dawn of the constitutional republic. Another advantage is that, the impact of any state-level problems, such as fraud, is localized[58]. No political party can commit

---

[56] Ibid.
[57] Ibid.
[58] Ibid.

large-scale fraud in any one state to dramatically influence an election[59]. The reason for claiming that the Electoral College is an effective electoral system is because it forces candidates to structure their campaign in a specific way: they focus on about a dozen swing states such as Florida, Ohio, Wisconsin, New Hampshire, Virginia, Iowa, and North Carolina[60]. Republicans waste no resources campaigning in decidedly blue states like Washington, Oregon or California, while Democrats avoid campaigning in red states like Texas, Georgia, and Oklahoma[61].

The Electoral College is evidently encapsulated in the Constitution of the United States. The Constitutional Convention of 1787 considered several methods of electing the President, including selection by Congress, by the governors of the states, by the states legislatures, by a special group of Members of Congress chosen by

---

[59] Ibid.
[60] Ibid.
[61] Ibid.

lot, and by direct popular election[62]. The method of direct popular election was discredited because the United States was not founded upon a direct democracy. Popular vote would have perfectly functioned at a small scale of government. Notwithstanding, the United States was designed to be republic constructed under federalism with a legislature empowered to ensure the sovereignty of every state that encompasses the federation. The Constitution gave each state a number of electors equal to the combined total of its membership in the Senate and its delegation in the House of Representatives[63]. The intent behind that redistribution was to reconcile differing state and federal interests, provide a degree of popular participation in the election, give less populous states some additional leverage in the process by providing senatorial electors, preserve the presidency as independent of Congress, and

---

[62] "Electoral College" www.history.com. Article. Web.
[63] Ibid.

66

generally insulate the election process from political manipulation[64].

In the Electoral College system, the electors are the guardians of the public will. It alludes that, as independent actors, they pledge to solely vote for the candidate that the party has nominated[65]. The Electoral College is authenticated in the Constitution under the Twelfth Amendment. Undeniably, the Twelfth Amendment requires electors to meet in their respective states for the sake of deterring political manipulation[66]. The benefits of the Electoral College come from the need to win state-by-state[67]. It is a very democratic process. The voter determines how his state will cast his vote. In my opinion, the continuation of the Electoral College is a vital element of the American political order. Dismantling the Electoral College would long-term destabilize the political order that

---

[64] Ibid.

[65] Ibid.

[66] Ibid.

[67] England, Trent, "The Electoral College Serves The Interests of All People". *US News,* Nov. 2012. www.usnews.com Article. Web.

has always secured and perpetuated the
foundations of American democracy.

Part II
On Foreign Policy

VI.

On American
Foreign Policy

Foreign policy is an intrinsic element of the American political order. Foreign policy is embodied in the political order because a modern state ought to have diplomatic relations with its neighbors or any other sovereign power. The philosophical backbone of American foreign policy is ascertained between non-interventionism and interventionism. It is hard to assert that American foreign policy is determined by exactly one trend. In fact, the evolution of the American republic upon the international scale has demonstrated that American foreign policy shifts based upon the course of events. The United States has evolved from being a non-interventionist nation to a more interventionist power. The pivotal point of this drastic alteration was undeniably World War II.

Prior to World War II, United States' foreign policy was centralized on isolationism. Isolationism is a policy or doctrine institutionalized by leaders who assert that their nation's best interests are served by keeping the affairs of other countries at a distance[68]. The isolationist perspective dates to the colonial days[69]. The first president of the United States, George Washington, in his farewell speech, accentuated his foreign policy vision upon the need for the United States to adopt a more reluctant attitude toward foreign nations. Washington believed that the isolationism of the United States would help the republic focusing on domestic policy, which means that the government would spend its economic resources on the advancement of American societal needs. The United States remained politically isolated all through the 19th century and the beginning of the 20th century, an unusual feat in western history[70]. One of the advantages of this unusual feat is ingrained in the fact that the United States is geographically subtracted from European Powers because of the Atlantic Ocean. During the 1930s, the combination of the Great Depression and the memory of tragic

---

[68] Wikipedia Contributors. "Isolationism" Wikipedia, The Free Encyclopedia, August 19, 2018. Web.
[69] "Isolationism" U.S. History. www.u-s-history.com. Article
[70] Ibid.

loss in World War I, contributed to pushing American public opinion and policy toward isolationism[71]. Isolationists advocated non-involvement in European and Asian conflicts and non-entanglement in international politics[72]. The reality of a worldwide economic depression and the need for an increased attention to domestic problems only served to bolster the idea that the United States isolated itself from troubling events in Europe[73]. During the interwar period (1919-1941), the United States government repeatedly chose non-entanglement over participation or intervention as the appropriate response to international questions[74].

Contrariwise, December 7, 1941, is the date that utterly shaped the fate of American foreign policy. The attacks on Pearl Harbor from the Japanese Empire gave no choice to the United States but to enter World War II. The United States'

---

[71] "American Isolationism in the 1930s". *Office of the Historian*, www.history.state.gov. Article.
[72] Ibid.
[73] Ibid.
[74] Ibid.

entrance into the Second World War compelled the federal government to embrace an interventionist attitude after the war. Incrementally, the adjudicating factor that constrained the United States to remain interventionist throughout the 20th century, was the expansion of the Soviet Union over the Eastern European countries and its threat as a communist superpower. By defeating Nazi Germany, and liberating western European countries, the United States became the leader of the "free world", and consequently, the superpower of the western hemisphere. The United States could, therefore, not withdraw from its role as the world's leader, and as the defender of freedom against communism, so it could not return to an isolationist foreign policy. The fall of the Berlin Wall in 1989 and the dissolution of the Union of Soviet Socialist Republics in 1991, inevitably entitled the United States to become the only great superpower. Hence, the United States as the unique superpower, had to the responsibility to conduct an interventionist foreign policy in its quest to ensure and preserve peace around the world.

As we now live in the twenty-first century, a century in which the United States is unequivocally the greatest economic and military power in the world, it is unconditionally nonsensical for the United States to re-adopt isolationism as its main foreign policy philosophy as Donald Trump has been suggesting. The federal government has received critics over its numerous military interventions. Nonetheless, I believe that it is the role of the United States as the sole superpower, to ensure peace in territories that it deems having political and economic interests. It is, nevertheless, significant to fathom that American foreign interventions shall be limited solely to humanitarian needs. The United States government had militarily intervened in foreign conflicts for diverse reasons, and its extensive military interventions placed the United States in a more imperialistic position than as an advocate of peace. As far as I know, American military interventions have engendered more harm to foreign nations than ensuring peace. For this purpose, is it essential that American interventionism in foreign policy, be regulated strictly to humanitarian demands. The use of military might must be exhausted only as last resort, when negotiation and diplomatic relations have failed to solve whatsoever conflicts.

VII.

On American Expansionism

Being in favor of interventionism does not mean that I support expansionism. In fact, I am vehemently opposed to American expansionism in this century (21st century). As a matter of fact, expansionism is imperialism, and imperialism is the epitome of colonization. American expansionism in the twenty-first century is purely and simply imperialism, and imperialism is the violation of sovereignty. American expansionism has been camouflaged under the guise of "spreading of democracy around the world". This idea of spreading democracy around the world has been promoted by Former U.S. President George W. Bush, Former U.S. Vice President Richard Bruce Cheney, Former Secretary of Defense Donald Rumsfeld, and Former Deputy Secretary of Defense Paul Wolfowitz. These four government officials enhanced the neoconservative movement.

The principal different between neoconservatism and paleoconservatism is entrenched in their approach to foreign policy. Paleoconservatives are proponents of isolationism. Neoconservatives, however, favored a staunch interventionism. Indeed, neoconservatism believes that American greatness is measured by our willingness to be a great power—through vast and virtually unlimited global military involvement[75]. Substantially, neoconservatism advocates for an active interventionism, in shaping the world order because if it refrains from doing so, then the world order will be shaped by other powers, other nations, in ways that might be inimical to the interests and ideals of the United States[76]. Noted that George W. Bush, Richard B. Cheney, Donald Rumsfeld, and Paul Wolfowitz did not create the neoconservative movement. They simply patronized it. Neoconservatism is rooted in post-World War II. Neoconservatism began to emerge in the later 1960s when liberal intellectuals began to consider   the

---

[75] Hunter, Jack, "What's a Neoconservative?" *The American Conservative.* June 23, 2011, www.theamericanconservative.com. Article. Web.
[76] Vaisse, Justin, "Neoconservatism and American Foreign Policy". *Brookings.* August 2010, www.brookings.edu. Article. Web.

lessons of the decades' fail reforms[77]. The social disorder and urban riots of the mdi-and late 1960s led some liberals, particularly Moynihan, and Kristol, to new appreciation of the role of institutions and traditional authority in society[78]. These liberals commenced to drift to the right, with a vision on foreign policy that would heavily rely upon militaristic means to promote America's greatness.

I am tenaciously opposed to neoconservatism because it has corroborated to be more detrimental than benign to foreign policy and to American society generally speaking. The Iraq War is a flawless example of the nuisance of neoconservatism. At the outset of this essay, I have ingeminated that imperialism is a violation of sovereignty. Saddam Hussein was indubitably a terrible human being and a ruthless political leader. As Iraq's strongman, he deprived his people of their most elementary rights as individuals living in a civil

---

[77] Ehrman, John, "Neoconservatism" *First Principles.* November 2011, www.firstprinciplesjournal.com Article. Web.
[78] Ibid.

society. It is undeniable that the political situation was catastrophic. Was this chaotic political situation legitimated for the United States to militarily intervene in Iraq and overthrow Saddam? Absolutely not. It was not up to the United States to intervene in Iraq to save the Iraqi people from its tyrant, but solely to the Iraqi people (theoretically at least). The power of popular sovereignty is mightier than any obstacle that a civil society could ever encounter because the people are the one that substantiate civil society. There are three main reasons that clearly demonstrate the illegitimated American intervention in Iraq.

The first reason is grounded in the absolutism of the Iraqi popular sovereignty. Truthfully, Iraqi civil society was not designed upon the precept of liberal democracy as we understand it here in the West. Arab civil societies, especially Iraqi civil society, have been designed under an authoritative political order. This political order is established in the leader who would be the absolute decider. Iraqi political order can be explained upon the theory of Hobbes. They consent to a leader who would be the ultimate decider of all political, economic, and social decisions. In exchange, the leader, or the sovereign is merely obligated to ensure for the safety of the state and the welfare of its people. Under the tyranny of Saddam Hussein, the Iraqi people were surely not politically free as we would fathom here, but Iraq was safe and its economy was not as bad as it was pretended. If the Iraqi people were truly disgruntled with the regime of Saddam, they would have found a way and the means to overthrow his [Saddam] regime, because the will of the people is ultimate and unshakeable. The civil overthrow of Hosni Mubarak in Egypt in 2011 is the perfect illustration of the power of popular sovereignty. The dissatisfaction of the Egyptian people pressured Mubarak to resigned after thirty years of solitary rule. The Iraqi people did not desperately cry out for democracy as the Bush administration portrayed it. The military intervention in Iraq that led to the overthrow of Saddam Hussein was a limpid violation of the sovereignty of Iraq. It was not the Iraqi people who removed Saddam from power but the United States, a foreign power, hostile to Iraq—that did so. The United States removed Saddam Hussein from power without the consent of the Iraqi People and without the consent of the United Nations. This military intervention had the sole purpose to expand the military and political power of the United States in the Middle East, which is to me, an act of expansionism rather than a genuine act of upbringing "freedom" to a nation that did not ask for it.

The second reason of the illegitimated American intervention in Iraq is grounded in the unliteral action of the United States government to intercede in Iraq without the consent of the United Nations. The United Nations is the largest world's organization that works to promote and ensure peace around the world including by force. That is why the United Nations has an armed forces compare to the League of Nations which fail to secure peace through strength after World War I. For the United States government to have the legal authority to invade Iraq, the permanent members of the United Nations Security Council had to unanimously agree. France, Russia, and the People's Republic of China did not find any substantive legal precept that would justify the United States' intervention in Iraq. They logically opposed any form of military intervention in Iraq. Only the United Kingdom agreed to accompany the United States government in its imperialistic intervention. The overthrow of Saddam Hussein was not an intervention, it was an invasion. Any form of invasion is synonym of imperialism and colonization.

The third and final reason of the illegitimated American intervention in Iraq is based upon the tremendous falsehood that the Bush administration has profaned to justify its invasion in Bagdad. The Bush administration falsely claimed that the Iraqi government possessed weapons of mass destruction. As any sovereign power that aims to pursue an imperialistic agenda, the United States under the Bush administration needed an excuse to go to war for the sake of expanding its power. This false claims from the Bush administration misled the American people and plunged the country into a war that cost many casualties and accumulated the national debt which outbroke the world's economic crisis of 2008. Furthermore, the illegitimated intervention in Iraq created a religious war between Muslims and Christians. Christian Americans became increasingly distrustful of Muslims Americans since former President George W. Bush in his State of the Union speech of 2003 used the terms such as "good versus evil" and "axe of evil" to describe the regime of Saddam Hussein and Islam, and "forces of good" to imply the superiority of the Christian religion over the Islamic faith.

The United States may have won the Iraq War militarily because Iraq does not have the same artillery as those of the United States, but the United States has lost this war because it has failed to implement democracy as it said it would do. The invasion in Iraq brought desolation, chaos, and the destabilization of the Middle East. Democracy is not the kind of regime to impose on one another. For democracy to work, the people must primarily understand what it means to be free in a politically organized society. Secondly, they must comprehend the significance of these political liberties that they are entitled to. The Iraqi people were not at that stage yet to embrace democracy. The failure to incorporate democracy in Iraq has portrayed the United States as an imperialistic power that is only driven by expanding. These reasons are why I will always be a staunch opponent of American expansionism in foreign policy.

VIII.

On Military Spending

When it comes to military spending, the question has always been to know if the military budget should be augmented or diminished. For a nation like the United States, a nation in possession of more than seven thousands nuclear weapons; military spending is momentous for maintaining the strength of the of the armed forces. As the strongest military power in contemporary history, the United States government is, I assert, morally obligated to increase its military budget. The moral duty is founded in the fact that the United States' economy cannot flourish if the safety of its citizens are not primarily secured. In the 2016 Republican Primary Debate, United States Senator, Marco Rubio declared that the economic growth of the United States cannot thrive unless its safety is retained.

To understand how much we ought to spend on the military, we first need to get a handle on what exactly we want our military to be capable of doing[79].

---

[79] Salam, Reiham, "The United States Doesn't Spend Enough on Its Military". *Slate.* November 2015. www.slate.com. Article.

There is a large and growing gap between what we expect of our military and what it can realistically accomplish[80]. Many Americans believe that what we really ought to do is to lower our expectations for what our military should be able to accomplish, which in turn would allow the United States to spend less[81]. The truth is that, an augmentation of military expenditures is necessary for three reasons.

The first and foremost reason is to ensure peace and safety for our citizens through strength. Certainly, since September 11, 2001, the level of danger and threat from a foreign power has commensurably curtailed because the United States government has increased its military budget in order to create programs that would play a preventive role in the preservation of peace and safety. Despite the terrible debacle of the Iraq War that caused enormous casualties abroad and the loss of the majority of our soldier, the Bush administration played, nonetheless, a decisive role in enhancing domestic safety through preemptive

---

[80] Ibid.
[81] Ibid.

war. The idea of preemptive or preventive war is rooted in the anticipation of imminent foreign attacks that could damage the sovereignty of the state and endangered the safety of the citizens of the United States. A strong military budget was, thenceforward, compulsory to secure domestic peace.

The second reason that motivates me to advocate for a strong military is grounded into the leadership role that the United States holds in the western world. Since the dissolution of the Soviet Union, the United States became the incontestable and only superpower. It has ensured peace and political stability in the most part of Europe. Many former Soviet satellite states have endorsed the capitalistic views of the United States because they were seeking economic prosperity. By entering into NATO, countries like Turkey, Romania, Poland and many other Eastern European countries consented to follow the leadership of the United States in exchange for military protection through the implementation of military bases. The effectuation of these military bases in each of these countries deters any invasion attempt from the Russian counterpart. The United States shall retain its leadership in Eastern Europe by way of increasing military budget to insure the protection of these nations. Additionally, protecting these nations militarily decreases the number of potential enemies.

The third reason for supporting an augmentation of the military budget is ingrained in the extent of military superiority. The superiority of the United States is determined by its military might. It is important to remember the extent to which peace depends on overwhelming military superiority on multiple fronts, from Europe to East Asia[82]. Countries like Iran, or North Korea have intrinsically expanded their nuclear arsenal over the years, and are now a true military menace to the United States. Yet, their [Iran & North Korea] military arsenal does not equate those of the United States, it is quintessential that the United States counters

---

[82] French, David, "Yes, It is Time to Increase Defense Spending". *National Review*, February 27, 2017. www.nationalreview.com. Article. Web.

and contains its military growth to in order to obliviate any further threat. The deployment of peer or near-peer equipment by potential hostile powers could be destabilizing unless we maintain our generational edge in equipment and sufficient numbers of troops to engage foes with decisive forces[83]. National defense is a core constitutional function of government, and other agencies can sacrifice to maintain American deterrence[84].

---

[83] Ibid.
[84] Ibid.

IX.

On Foreign Spending

As the United States has imposed itself as the leading nation of the western world, and the only superpower remaining after the dissolution of the Soviet Union, it is therefore logical that the United States conceives a budget on foreign economic assistance, more simply known as foreign aid. The far-right has claimed that the United States government has spent an extensive amount of financial resources on foreign governments, and that, it is wherefore time that the government focuses its expenses on the American people. If we categorically cut off our foreign budget, the United States will undeniably lose its influence and prevalence over its allies and the countries that support our policies.

I believe that the United States should, and must increase its budget on foreign spending. It is vital for our own economy and fundamental for the preservation of our influence. Those in favor of promoting 'America First' shall primarily fathom that foreign aid strengthens America diplomatic ties with foreign nations on the economic scale, and make the United States even safer. Surveys have shown that many Americans assume that the country spends upwards of 20 percent of the federal budget on foreign aid.[85] In reality, nonmilitary foreign assistance—including all of America's work on international development and global heath—represents less than 1 percent of the federal budget[86]. For less than 1 percent of the federal budget, the United States led a global coalition to fight HIV/AIDS when the disease threatened to devastate and destabilize much of the African continent[87]. The creation of program assistances on foreign aid demonstrate that the United States truly leads by example and attempts to safeguard peace in the most fragile regions of the world. In 2016, President Obama implemented one of the largest foreign aid programs. The program is called the President's Emergency Plan for AIDS

---

[85] Michael Garson, Raj Shah, "America First Shouldn't Mean Cutting Foreign Aid." *The Washington Post.* February 24, 2017. www.washingtonpost.com. Article. Web.
[86] Ibid.
[87] Ibid.

Relief (PEPFAR)[88]. The program, which President Bush started in 2003, has a clear humanitarian and health benefits for people around the world[89]. This program has transformed the global HIV/AIDS response by supporting nearly 11.5 million people with antiretroviral treatment, and nearly 2 million babies have been born HIV-free to pregnant women living with HIV[90]. Comprehensively, the implementation of this program has saved millions of lives in Africa and elsewhere. If we did not accentuate our foreign aid, those people would have been condemned to die because they would not have the adequate resources to fight incurable diseases like cancer and HIV, and would have not been able to invest in sanitization. Programs like PEPFAR promote economic growth across the American economy by building strong foreign markets for American goods[91].

---

[88] Cumbo, Peter, "Foreign Aid: Good For America, Good For The World", *Public Policy Initiative.* Wharton, University of Pennsylvania. July 9, 2017. www.publipolicy.wharton.upenn.edu. Article.
[89] Ibid.
[90] Ibid.
[91] Ibid.

I believe that the United States government should increase its humanitarian foreign aid and lessen its military foreign spending. Do not misunderstand what I am implying. I support the idea of a strong military. I have enumerated the reasons that dictate my choice in the previous essay *On Military Spending.* The augmentation of the military budget that I am in favor of is strictly to reinforce the purposes of our national defense. I am opposed to the fact that the United States government spends a considerable amount of the military budget on foreign military assistance. In 2015, the United States alone spent $12.4 billion on foreign military assistance. Afghanistan received $4.5 billion, Israel accepted $3.7 billion, Iraq acquired $1.8 billion, Egypt welcomed $1.3 billion, and Pakistan was the beneficiary of $1.1 billion[92]. Notwithstanding this fact, the foreign economic assistance budget was not converted into billions like the military one. Indeed, Kenya received $763 million, $650 million for Ethiopia, $646 million for

---

[92] Tremblay-Boire, "US Foreign Aid Explained" *The Conversation.* www.theconversation.com. Article. Web.

Nigeria, and $633 million for Tanzania[93]. Each of these countries citied received less than a billion dollar in foreign assistance. I hold that the United States must increment its foreign aid, abate its military assistance to foreign governments, and reinforce meticulously its military budget exclusively for national defense purposes. It is more substantial to assist foreign powers economically than militarily. The United States spends very little on foreign aid relative to the size of its economy, particularly compared to other rich countries.[94] As congress decided whether to follow Trump's lead by slashing foreign aid spending, lawmakers should take into account the fact that taxpayers already spend far less than our global peers on foreign aid[95].

---

[93] Ibid.
[94] Ibid.
[95] Ibid.

X.

On NATO and the United Nations

The North Atlantic Treaty Organization known as NATO, was created in 1949 by the United States, Canada, and several western European nations to provide collective security against the Soviet Union[96]. The United States viewed an economically strong, rearmed and integrated Europe as vital to the prevention of communist expansion across the continent[97]. As a result, Secretary of State George Marshall proposed a program of large-scale economic aid to Europe[98]. The resulting recovering program, or the Marshall Plan, did not only facilitated European economic integration, but promoted the idea of shared interests and cooperation between the United States and Europe[99].

The fall of the Berlin Wall in 1989, and the dissolution of the Soviet Union in 1991, reinforced the authenticity of NATO. However, the proponents

---

[96] North Atlantic Treaty Organization (NATO). 1949", *Office of The Historian.* www.history.state.gov. Article.
[97] Ibid.
[98] Ibid.
[99] Ibid.

of isolationism assert that NATO is an expansionist organization that was created by the United States to entrench its domination. The isolationists asseverated that—maintaining the existence of NATO with the participation of the United States within the organization exacerbates the federal budget of the United States government. Conservative NATO skeptics tend to bring two types of criticism against the organization[100]. They [conservative skeptics] view NATO membership as a concession of the United States sovereignty and agency[101]. Taking part in a mutual defense pact means the United States is having to defend other countries in ways that run contrary to its own interests[102]. The second criticism describes the problem in financial terms. The United States cannot afford to spend the money it does not have on NATO[103]. The Left or the liberal skeptics on the

----

[100] Bonenberger, Adrian, "Against NATO: The Other Side of The Argument". *The Wrath-Bearing Tree.* October 2016, www.wrath-bearingtree.com. Article. Web.
[101] Ibid.
[102] Ibid.
[103] Ibid.

matter, is less concerned about advancing United States interests, and more interested in expanding a world where people can live free from war[104]. The Left believes that a smaller or a non-existent NATO would inevitably lead to a more peaceful world[105]. The leftist tends to believe that the lack of education, and civic morality leads to misunderstanding and violence[106].

The argument of the skeptical on both side of the political spectrum is comprehensible. Nonetheless, I disagree with their rationale although they have a fair point. I do not perceive NATO as an expansionist military organization. I am against expansionism of the United States government when it wages war of aggression against nations that are militarily weak, such as Iraq or Afghanistan. Calling NATO an expansionist organizational power led by the United States would imply that the European members of the organization have been coerced to subordinate their sovereignty to the

---

[104] Ibid.
[105] Ibid.
[106] Ibid.

United States. It is manifestly not the case. The European members of NATO voluntarily abided to join the organization in order to strengthen their own national security. I hold that it is quintessential to maintain NATO because it principally upholds peace in the western hemisphere and deters Russia from acquiring more European territories. The fundamental benefit for sustaining NATO is that it remains a preventive mechanism[107]. It was an effort to keep the world from collapsing into global conflict[108]. The collaborative deterrent power of NATO is what makes the bedrock of the international system that President Harry S. Truman built[109]. Sharing basis with our allies saves the United States, billions of dollars , and having troops around the world keeps our transportations costs down[110]. Strategically, the subsistence of NATO increases readiness, in including both lethality and effectiveness, and ensures interoperability, or the

---

[107] West, Graham, "The Benefits NATO" *Cagle.* July 12, 2018. www.cagle.com. Article. Web.
[108] Ibid.
[109] Ibid.
[110] Ibid.

technical compatibility of our forces and hardware[111].

The United Nations was created in 1945, following the defeat of Nazi Germany, and the Axis powers. The creation of the United Nations resulted from the carnage that shook Europe and the entire world. To avoid having an event such as World War II again, President Franklin D. Roosevelt, British Prime Minister Winston Churchill, and Soviet Premier Joseph Stalin conceived an organization that would retain peace in the world. An organization that would be more powerful than the League of Nations. The United Nations is composed of five nations that have permanent membership in the Security Council, and 190 other nations that member states of the world organization. The United States is among the five permanent members of the Security Council with the United Kingdom, the French Republic, the People's Republic of China, and the Russian Federation. Being part of the Security Council insinuates that whatever nation

---

[111] Ibid.

member of that council possess decisive powers that would utterly shape the fate of a contingency. The prevalent debate among Americans is to know if the United States shall dwell to be a member of the United Nations. Many Americans avouch the argument that the United States shall withdraw from the United Nations. But once again, it is the isolationists who are insisting upon that thinking. They sustained that argument upon the basis that the United Nations is useless and does not serve the interests of the United States. I think the contrary. I do even believe that it would be a terrible decision if the United States withdraws from the Union Nations.

I conjecture that the United Nations is still relevant to the United States' interests. There are two principal reasons that, I believe, are necessary for the sustenance of the United States in the organization. First and foremost, the United States shall stay in the United Nations for humanitarian reasons. The United Nations provides food to 90 million people in seventy-tree countries, and assist over 36 million refugees and people fleeing war, famine and persecution[112]. The United States contributes to enhance the humanitarian branch of the United Nations. The United States alone supplies one percent of its budget to assist foreign governments economically. The United States dedicates 22 percent of its federal budget to the United Nations whereby 10 percent goes on endowing humanitarian and economic growth. The second argument is rooted on security basis. The United States is the biggest contributor to peacekeeping among the members of the Security Council. The United States utilizes 28 percent of its budget to promote peacekeeping policies for the United Nations to keep on going. Moreover, as a permanent member of the United Nations Security Council, the United States ultimately has the final say over the size of the peacekeeping budget[113]. By bestowing more than the four other permanent members of the security council to the

---

[112] Vanden Heuvel, Katrina, "More Than Ever, We Need The UN" *The Nation.* February 20, 2013. www.thenation.com. Article.
[113] "Importance of Funding The UN" *US-UN Partnership.* www.betterworldcamapign.org. Article.

110

peacekeeping budget, the United States substantiates the validity of its leadership as the world peacekeeper or "the world policeman". Omit the Iraq War in which the United States government went to war unilaterally under the Bush administration, the United States have usually acted multilaterally to preserve peace around the world[114].

---

[114] Multilateralism is a political doctrine in international politics that stipulates the implementation of a particular policy through the consent and mutual agreement of several sovereign nations. Multilateralism is opposed to unilateralism.

Part III
On Immigration Law

XI.

On The Deferred Action for Childhood Arrivals (DACA)

The Deferred Action for Childhood Arrivals (DACA) is an American immigration policy that allows some individuals who were brought to the United States illegally as children to receive a renewable two-year period of deferred action from deportation and become eligible for a work permit in the United States[115]. On June 15, 2012, then-Secretary of Homeland Security Janet Napolitano, issued a memorandum entitled *"Exercising Prosecutorial Discretion with Respect to Individuals Who Came To The United States as Children"*, creating a non-congressional authorized administrative program that permitted certain individuals who came to the United States as juveniles and meet several criteria including lacking any lawful immigration status[116].

DACA states a set of requirements that are necessary to confirm the eligibility of an individual within the program. Any individual, precisely the

---

[115] Wikipedia Contributors, "Deferred Action for Childhood Arrivals" Wikipedia, the Free Encyclopedia, September 8, 2018.

[116] "Deferred Action for Childhood Arrivals (DACA)" Department of Homeland Security, June 23, 2018. Commentary. www.dhs.gov.

children of illegal aliens, who wishes to apply to DACA relief shall primarily be under 31 years of age as of June 15, 2012, must have arrived in the United States under age 16, and ought to have continuously resided in the United States from June 15, 2007[117]. Furthermore, the requirements' guideline stipulate that an individual seeking to apply for DACA shall have entered the United States without inspection or fell out of lawful visa status before June 15, 2012; shall be going currently in school, including graduating high school with the obtainment of a GED[118]. Finally, the individual applying for DACA's eligibility essentially need to have not been convicted of any felony offense, a significant misdemeanor, or more than three misdemeanors of any kind[119]. Conclusively, the DACA applicant shall not pose a threat to national security or public safety[120]. As President Obama initiated the program,

---

[117] "DACA (Deferred Action for Childhood Arrivals)"*Immigration Equality.* 2015. www.immigrationequality.org. Commentary
[118] Ibid.
[119] Ibid.
[120] Ibid.

the primary intent of the effectuation of DACA was to provide to illegal aliens, an opportunity to legally settle in the United States. Unlike the Dreamer Act which offered a path to citizenship but failed to pass in Congress, DACA does not propose a path to citizenship. It helps, nonetheless, the illegal alien child to lawfully work under a work permit, and provide for his family.

The Trump administration has manifested a steadfast opposition to the program. President Donald Trump, with the support of his Attorney General, Jefferson Beauregard Sessions III, has intended to terminate the program. Opponents of DACA, besides their argument that it rewarded illegal immigration, claimed that the implementation of DACA was beyond the power of the President [Obama] and his administration[121]. Proponents of anti-immigration reform affirmed that the effectuation of DACA was the expansion of federal authority without legislative process. The Trump administration is asking the United States

---

[121] Kopan, Tal, "What Is DACA And Why Is It Ending?" *CNN Politics*, January 2, 2018, www.cnn.com. Article. Web.

Supreme Court to intervene in a federal case to allow President Donald Trump to end an immigration program for hundreds of thousands of children who were brought to America illegally by their parents[122]. The Supreme Court' order and the previous judicial rulings keep the Trump administration from ending the program on March 5, 2018, but around one hundred DACA recipients have been losing their work permits and deportation deferrals every day[123].

As a green card holder, and therefore a United States permanent resident, I legally came in the United States under a student visa within an alien status. Consequently, I personally comprehend the struggle of those who are seeking legal status in order to live and experiment the American Dream. As an immigrant myself, it would be hypocritical from myself to support DACA's

---

[122] Lanktoree, Graham, "Trump Administration Calls On Supreme Court To End DACA". *Newsweek,* January 19, 2018. www.newsweek.com. Article. Web
[123] Rhodan Maya, "When Does DACA Expire? The Supreme Court Just Gave Dreamers More Time", *Time,* February 26, 2018, www.time.com. Article. Web.

termination. I do stand for the preservation of DACA. I believe that the Deferred Action for Childhood Arrivals shall be maintained. The Obama administration has deported more illegal immigrants than any other administration in United States history. More than two million illegal immigrants have been deported under the governance of President Obama. Notwithstanding, the Obama administration fathomed that minors brought in the United States illegally should not be at fault for literally existing and wanting to pursue a better life in their current surroundings[124]. Whereas DACA was effectuated by executive order, it reflects the principles of the American Dream. It demonstrates the core of American values—those values that I deeply believe in.

The United States is a nation that embraces cultural diversity and the precepts of liberty, ideologically and practically. Cultural diversity is constitutionally enforced in the First Amendment

---

[124] Fitzgerald, Kiana, "Here's What DACA Is And Why It's So Important". *Complex.* September 2017, www.complex.com. Article. Web.

via the religious liberties clause. I am convinced that every single non-American child or teenager living in the United States and registered under DACA is a potential force that would contribute to American societal advancement. It is substantial to give to the illegal children and teenagers, the opportunity to create a life for themselves as the motto of American values accentuates it. Nevertheless, I do advocate for DACA to be transcended from an executive order into a legislation. If DACA is subjected to the legislative process, which means it [DACA] is considered as a legislative bill then voted to become law, it will henceforth substantiate and define a new comprehensive immigration reform that would certainly dignify the image and reputation of the United States around the world. It is quintessential that Republicans and Democrats utilize a bipartisan approach to ensure the sustentation of the Deferred Action for Childhood Arrivals. We must not disregard the fact that the United States is chiefly a nation of immigrants known for its hospitality and its tenacity for vindicating law and order.

XII.

On The Border Wall

During the 2016 presidential elections, Donald Trump emerged as the greatest element of surprise in American politics. He distinguished himself from the conventional politicians by his vulgarity, abrasiveness, arrogance, unfiltered vocabulary, and hateful rhetoric. Unlike his political opponents such as Governor John Kasich of Ohio, and Governor John Ellis Bush of Florida who proposed an allegedly "weak" immigration reform to halt illegal immigration, Donald Trump initiated the idea of building a border wall on the Southern border if he were to become President of the United States of America. The Border Wall was unequivocally the most unconventional thought ever enunciated upon a presidential bid. Donald Trump made of the idea of the Border Wall, the principal axis of his political platform. This extreme idea was later adopted by the Republican Party once Donald Trump became the party's nominee. The main question about the Border Wall is to know whether its construction is the adequate solution to the prevention of illegal immigrants.

The President of the United States [Trump] is phlegmatically convinced that building the Wall will prohibit illegal immigration. Border-security experts argue that while walls may be an impediment to migrants attempting to cross into a country, their purpose is usually largely symbolic[125]. If built, the construction of this wall would reflect the symbol of white American nationalism and bigotry. Officials from the Departments of Homeland Security and Justice argued that the nation would not have to spend money detaining people who illegally crossed the border if a barrier was built[126]. In 2016, Donald Trump insulted a federal judge due to his Mexican heritage. This judge is Judge Gonzalo Curiel. In 2018, Judge Gonzalo Curiel ruled in favor of the Trump administration to build the wall. He based his ruling upon the principle that the court does not and shall not consider whether underlying decisions

---

[125] Alvarez, Priscilla, "The Border Wall Prototypes Are Up-Now What?" *The Atlantic.* Oct. 26, 2017, www.theatlantic.com. Article. Web
[126] Shelbourne, Mallory, "Trump Officials Make Case For Border Wall". *The Hill.* December, 21, 2017. www.thehill.com. Article. Web.

to construct the Border Wall is politically wise or prudent[127]. Whereas President Trump may have received legal authority to build the wall, his administration does still not have the fund to build it.

When it comes to immigration policy, I have always favored strong immigration policies founded on a merit-based. However, I do not believe that building a wall on the southern border would or will utterly preclude illegal immigration. The reality is that—the majority of "illegal" immigrants come legally in the United States, then overstay. It is their overstay that shift their immigration status from "legal" to "illegal". Politically, I think building the wall is a treason to American values and does not enforce safety. It is a treason because it betrays the fundamentals principles of human rights and dignity that the American political culture has always upheld. The construction of this wall would symbolize the rise of totalitarianism in America.

---

[127] Rainey, James, "Federal Judge Whom Trump Called 'Mexican' Clears Way For Border Wall". *NBC News.* February 27, 2018, www.nbcnews.com. Article. Web.

Totalitarian regimes are generally politically isolated, and the Border Wall will certainly confirm the isolation that the Trump administration is attempting to drag the United States into. There are practical considerations that would make the construction of the Wall incrementally difficult. A wall would probably be less easily damaged by man or nature, but in at least some areas, its impassibility could also become a maintenance liability[128]. Border Patrol agents have told Fox News that a border wall would still have allowed water to pass through, or sheer force of raging water could damage its integrity[129]. The biggest practical problem with a wall is its opacity—in fact, many Border Patrol agents oppose a concrete wall for precisely the reason that—seeing through a fence allows agents to anticipate and mobilize, prior to illegal immigrants climbing or cutting through the fence[130].

---

[128] Bier, David, "Why The Wall Won't Work" *Cato Institute*, May 2017, www.cato.org. Article. Web.
[129] Ibid.
[130] Ibid.

As a survey in May 2017 indicated, 57 percent of the American people believe that the Wall will hurt the economy[131]. The Trump administration has set aside $1.5 billion for border security[132], but a total of $12 billion is destined to the Wall's construction. These $12 billion is twenty times the budget of America's economic assistance on foreign aid. Using that amount of money from the taxpayer will be an enormous waste of resources for the realization of the Wall—a wall that will not completely preclude illegal immigration. Indeed, the broader economic costs of the Wall are detrimental to the United States' economy no matter what financing options the White House picks[133]. If for instance, the White House persisted with the idea of imposing a tax on imports from Mexico, it would significantly hurt American retailers[134].

---

[131] Salay, Mark, "Would Mexican-US. Border Wall Help or Hurt The Economy?" *Marketplace,* May 1st, 2017. www.marketplace.org. Article. Web.
[132] Ibid.
[133] Felbab-Brown, Vanda, "Why the Border Wall's Costs for Outweigh Its Benefits". *Brookings.* January 30, 2017. www.brookings.edu. Article. Web.
[134] Ibid.

Furthermore, Mexican citizens could retaliate by boycotting American companies that operate in Mexico, such as Wal-Mart or Starbucks[135]. Finally, such boycotts could send the shares and profits of American companies plummeting, negatively affecting jobs, taxes, and the economy[136]. Contrary to its proclaimed aim of making America secure, the Wall has the potential to subvert American security—if Mexico stopped cooperating with the United States in going after violent criminal groups and drug cartels, the United States would be much worst[137].

---

[135] Ibid.
[136] Ibid.
[137] Ibid.

XIII.

On The Diversity Visa Program

The Diversity Visa Program became a major topic in the subject of immigration within the recent years, as mass immigration substantially augmented spasmodically. The Diversity Immigrant Visa Program was established under the Immigration Act of 1990 and administered by the State Department. Enacted on November 29, 1990, the Immigration Act of 1990 was an amendment in the United States immigration law that increased the number of legal immigrants that entered into the United States every year[138]. The main reason for its implementation was to change previous United States immigration law that prohibited the granting of visas to immigrants from certain countries[139]. Doubtlessly, the Diversity Visa Program promotes the liberal approach to immigration, which is what the concept of "nation of immigrants" was primarily based upon. Today, the issue of "Green Card Lottery" is within the heart of immigration issues. The Trump administration

---

[138] "The Immigration Act of 1990" Laws. www.immigration.laws.com. Commentary.
[139] Ibid.

and its chief [Donald Trump] championed for the discontinuation of the Diversity Visa Program.

The president [Trump] affirmed that the Diversity Visa Program was detrimental to American immigration laws and to the safety of the American people. Withal, the president asseverated that the Diversity Visa Program has generated loopholes in the immigration system because its [Diversity Visa Program] aleatory proceeding enables random foreigners, sometimes ill-intentioned individuals to easily enter the country and cause harm. The case of Sayfullo Habibulaevic Saipov is a perfect illustration to emphasize on the president's point. Sayfullo Saipov, an Uzbek national who entered the United States through the Diversity Visa Program, rented a pickup truck earlier and drove down to a busy bicycle path in the Manhattan area[140]. Authorities found a note in the truck claiming the attack was made in the ISIS and have since declared

---

[140] Goronja, Ariel, "Visa Lottery Program Needs Work, but Has American Value" *Media Milwaukee,* Students-Powered News. University of Wisconsin-Milwaukee. November 24, 2017, www.mediamilwaukee.com. Article. Web.

the incident as act of terror[141]. Proponents of the program's termination argue that it is flawed. In an opinion published on *The Hill*, Congressman Robert Goodlatte has communicated his dissatisfaction with the Diversity Visa Program. He asserted that usually, immigrant visas are issued to foreign nationals that have existing connections with family members lawfully residing in the United States or with American employers[142]. These types of relationships help ensure that immigrants entering the country have a stake in continuing America's success and have needed skills to contribute to the nation's economy[143]. I do agree with Congressman Goodlatte on that specific matter. I do also understand the argument of the president [Trump] although I do oppose its [Diversity Visa Program] termination.

---

[141] Ibid.

[142] Congressman Robert Goodlatte, "Visa Lottery Program Is Too Much of A Gamble For Our Nation And Needs To End" *The Hill,* November 6, 2017. www.thehill.com. Opinion. Web.

[143] Ibid.

I do not believe that the Diversity Visa Program shall be terminated. I, however, affirm that it shall be reformed. I conjecture that the Diversity Visa Program must change its procedure for the acquisition of the green card—and ought to thereafter, change its procedure for subsistence of the permanent residency. Prominently forward, I assert that the procedure for obtaining the green card must be reformed. It must be reformed in the sense that the procurement for the green card must be based upon a meritocratic system rather than an aleatory system whereby luck is principal factor of its acquisition. The merit-based system that I am advocating for shall be designed for immigrants that will for certain contribute to the economic growth of the United States. I believe that a set of conditions and requirements shall be met by the applicant who wants to obtain the green card through the Diversity Visa Program. These procedural requirements shall include an extensive background check that would elucidate the criminal record of the applicant, a financial status in good standing, a level of education acquired (at least the equivalent of a high school degree or GED), and other determining factors. He who wants to obtain the United States permanent residency shall work for it. Obtaining the United States permanent residency must be meritocratic rather than adventitious.

Reforming the green card acquisition process by strengthening its procedure is a good indicator to regulate the immigration system, and particularly the Diversity Visa Program. Adjunctively, I have also called for a reform upon the sustentation of the permanent residency in the United States. The very intent of the permanent residency is to allow the immigrant to be legally entitled to some fundamental rights such as the right to legally work for any employer, the right to afford a property, the right to take loans without the necessity of having an American sponsor, the right to sue individuals, private and public entities...etc., to basically create a life for himself or herself and to live the American dream.

Generally, a green card holder is not required to permanently live on American soil although he or she is a United States permanent resident. I find this policy repulsive and preposterous because it subverts the whole essence of the permanent residency. It makes the green card holder not being appreciative of the chances and opportunities he or she has in order to create wealth by living on American soil—chances and opportunities that he or she may not or would not have had if he or she was living in their homeland, wherein opportunities are scarce. I firmly believe that this policy should be repealed. A procedure of sustentation must be enforced upon green card holders. Under the current policy, a green card holder is still a permanent resident as long as the individual comes to the United States every six months, he or she is still a permanent resident. I believe that this policy ought to be abrogated. A permanent resident must demonstrate why he or she deserves to maintain his or her green card. The reasons illustrating why a permanent resident deserves to conserve his or her green card must be ingrained in a procedure that would encapsulate a set of conditions and prerequisites. These prerequisites must incorporate the factors that a permanent resident has been continuously living in the United States or in any territory subjected to the legal authority of the United States for at least twelve months without leaving the country, that the permanent resident has kept an untarnished criminal record, and that he or she has the financial resources to be self-sufficient. Some of the readers may find my views stringent on the matter, but I am convinced that it is a comprehensive and fair reform of immigration law that espouses the values of merit, excellence, quality, and worth. The United States has the most generous immigration system among all the industrial nations, with over one million of immigrants coming every year in the United States. European nations such as the United Kingdom, France, Sweden, Norway, and Germany do not have a system of diversity of lottery like we do here because they are trying restrain their immigration system. A green card holder shall be grateful to the United States, and for the opportunities he or she has as a permanent resident.

XIV.

On The United States Immigration and Customs Enforcement

The United States Immigration and Customs Enforcement (ICE) has been the subject of political discussion within this year 2018. Chiefly, the central idea of these debates rotated around the question to know if the Immigration and Customs Enforcement shall be abolished. Before getting to the heart of the subject, it is important that we first retrace the origins of the Immigration and Customs Enforcement.

The Immigration and Customs Enforcement was created in 2003, as part of the Department of Homeland Security after the September 11, 2001 attacks[144]. Within the establishment of the Department of Homeland Security, the immigration Customs and Enforcement is the largest investigative arm of the Department, and the second largest contributor to the nation's Joint Terrorism Task Force[145]. The Immigration and Customs

---

[144] Ron Nixon, Linda, Qin, "What Is ICE and Why Do Critics Want To Abolish it?" The New York Times. July 3, 2018. www.nytimes.com. Article. Web.

[145] Wikipedia Contributor, "US Immigration and Customs Enforcement": *Wikipedia*, The Free Encyclopedia, September 14, 2018. Web.

Enforcement is responsible for identifying and eliminating border, economic, transportation and infrastructure security vulnerabilities[146].

Under the Trump administration, many critics, especially liberals, are calling for the abolition of the Immigration and Customs Enforcement. Indeed, the Immigration and Customs Enforcement has been held in contempt for using unorthodox procedures toward illegal immigrants. The movement has been fueled by President Trump's divisive "zero tolerance" policy toward illegal immigrants, and the abhorrent practice of detaining immigrant children who have been separated from their parents[147]. The Immigration and Customs Enforcement has only existed for fifteen years[148]. The United States government spent $187 billion on immigration enforcement between 1990 and 2013 according to the Migration Policy Institute, deportations increased more than tenfold between 1990 and 2011, and the Immigration and

---

[146] Ibid.
[147] Steigerwald, Lucy, "The Case for Abolishing ICE". *The Week*, July 6, 2018, www.theweek.com. Article. Web.
[148] Ibid.

Customs Enforcement spends $2 billion every year to hold immigrants in private detention centers known for human rights abuse[149]. Some liberals go even further by asseverating that the abolition of the Immigration and Customs Enforcement would materially improve the lives of immigrants, who are by and large, a Democratic constituency[150]. Nonetheless, despite the fact that I do support DACA, I do, nonetheless, believe that abolishing the Immigration and Customs Enforcement would be a grotesque error of collective judgement. It is essential and imperative to maintain the Immigration and Customs Enforcement for several reasons.

Unlike other Western powers, the United States has a more or less generous immigration policy. If in addition to having a generous immigration system, we must abolish the Immigration and Customs Enforcement, then we are jeopardizing the safety of our fellow Americans.

---

[149] Ibid.
[150] Powell, Dominic, "How To Abolish ICE". *Jacobin*, June 29, 2018. www.jacobinmag.com. Article. Web.

Since the creation of the Immigration and Customs Enforcement, the United States has not been subjected to a direct foreign attack on American soil. Domestically, the Immigration and Customs Enforcement regulates the immigration system to an extent. The Enforcement and Removal Operations, the best-known division of ICE, arrests, detains and deports unauthorized immigrants already inside the United States[151]. Under President Barack Obama, the division has removed undocumented immigrants who had committed serious crimes in the United States[152]. Is the Immigration and Customs Enforcement the perpetrator of separating families at the border? Absolutely not. The perpetrator of this surely outrageous act is the Customs and Border Protection. The Customs and Border Protection is a parent agency for Border Patrol, which is responsible for patrolling , monitoring and securing

---

[151] Ron Nixon, Linda, Qin, "What Is ICE and Why Do Critics Want To Abolish it?" The New York Times. July 3, 2018. www.nytimes.com. Article. Web.
[152] Ibid.

the United States' borders with Canada and Mexico[153].

Furthermore, a significant portion of illegal immigrants are people who overstayed their visas—abolishing our internal-enforcement agency would mean that these illegal immigrants were de facto free to stay in the country so long as they did not commit a felony[154]. The fundamental issue about abolishing the Immigration and Customs Enforcement is that it is based on pure politics. It has no real substance. This issue is merely and purely words and an empty rhetoric by the liberal wing of the political spectrum. Liberals do plainly want the abolition of the Immigration and Customs Enforcement because they do not like the fact that President Donald Trump is in charge of the immigration laws of our country. I have reiterated the fact that President Obama, who is a liberal, has deported more illegal immigrants than Donald Trump, and any of his predecessors. When President

---

[153] Ibid.

[154] The Editors, "Don't Abolish ICE". *National Review*, July 6, 2018. www.nationalreview.com. Article. Web.

Obama utilized the Immigration and Customs Enforcement to enforce America's immigration laws, liberals and the tenors of the Democratic Party did not complain once. Today, these same people, shamelessly call for ICE's abolition because they would not be able to incorporate these immigrants into their political agenda in order to consolidate their political basis. In the eyes of Democrats and liberals, the Immigration and Customs Enforcement is an impediment that is endangering their political strategy since they use demography and identity politics to promulgate their political agenda.

Finally, the Immigration and Customs Enforcement must be maintained in order to enforce immigrations laws and to preserve the safety of the citizens. Abolishing the Immigration and Customs Enforcement would throw out a welcome mat for illegal immigrants, especially those who want to harm America[155]. There would be no effective enforcement of laws against potential

---

[155] Boyd, Kevin, "Here's Why Abolishing ICE Is A Terrible, Horrible, No Good, Very Bad Idea". *The Federalist,* July 11, 2018. www.thefederalist.com. Article. Web.

threats and crimes[156]. Whether Democratic leaders and lawmakers are pushing to eliminate the agency completely or simply restructure it[157], my personal thought on the matter is that, abolishing the Immigration and Customs Enforcement would be extremely foolish and injudicious. If it were to be replaced, the replacing agency would not be better or would not do a better job than what ICE is currently doing. Based on the Liberal platform (if the Democratic were to take back power), the agency that would replace the Immigration and Customs Enforcement will make of the immigration system a sieve, open to all the world's crises. The amount of illegal immigrants will triple and our immigration laws will lack foundation.

---

[156] Ibid.
[157] Godfrey, Elaine, "What 'Abolish ICE' Actually Means". *The Atlantic*, July 11, 2018, www.theatlantic.com. Article. Web.

Part IV
On Educational Policy

XV.

On the Privatization of
Public Education

The privatization of public education is the fundamental debate on educational policy in the United States. Before engaging the debate and arguing in a favor of a specific position, let's first comprehend what privatization of education means. Education privatization can be defined broadly as a process through which organizations and individuals participate increasingly and actively in a range of education activities and responsibilities that traditionally have been the remit of the state[158]. Education privatization is a process that tends to happen more at the level of provision and funding than at the level of ownership in a strict sense[159]. Nonetheless, privatization policies lean to generate opposition and political dispute[160]. The creation of the United States Department of Education in 1979, epitomizes the fact that for a very long time, since the establishment of the American republic,

---

[158] Antoni Verger, Clara Fontdevila, Adrian Zancaja, "The Privatization of Education: A Political Economy of Global Education Reform", *International Perspective On Education Reform*, (Teachers College Press, Columbia University. 2016) Article.
[159] Ibid.
[160] Ibid.

education was split between private actors and state governments. It was the Carter administration that generated the involvement of the federal government into education.

The adversarial argument to the privatization of public education sounds fair to an extent although I entirely disagree with its substance. Proponents of public education support public education because it promotes equality. Opponents of education privatization see the pressure for profit replacing student achievement as the driving force within schools[161]. They see individuals—particularly those of children with special costly requirements—being sacrificed to the needs of corporate shareholders[162]. Essentially, the opponents of the education privatization perceive its privatization as detrimental to the educational system. They argue that privatizing education

---

[161] Editorial Projects in Education Research Center (2004, October 4)"Issues A-Z: Privatization of Public Education" *Education Week.* September 19, 2018 from www.edweek.org/ew/issues/privatization-of-public-education/
[162] Ibid.

reflects the transactional aspect of businesses and corporations. According to their philosophy, privatizing education transcends conservative politics. Incrementally, they hold the belief that the *No Child Left Behind* of the Bush administration, and the *Race To The Top Fund* of the Obama administration are based on conservative world view of public education[163], which obstructs the concept of equality within the philosophy of public education. In each of these programs, it is only natural to think of education as a business[164]. Conclusively, opponents of education privatization claim that the privatization of public schools extract money out of the local community[165]. It takes hundreds of millions of dollars of taxpayer money out of the classroom that is instead spent on

---

[163] Hassard, Jack, "Why Education Must Be Public & Not Privatized", *The National Education Policy Center.* November 19, 2012, www.nepc.colorado.edu. Article. Web.

[164] Ibid.

[165] Hansen, Dale, "Privatization of Public Education Is A Failure", *The Huffington Post*, June 6, 2016. www.huffingtonpost.com. Article. Web.

154

advertising[166]. Although these arguments may have an adequate reasoning, I still disagree with the substance of argument.

The substance I am referring to is based upon the extent to which the government can enforce policies on educational matters. As a proponent of limited government, I do not believe that it is the role of the government to impose rules and regulations upon the kind of methods to educate my child. As we all know, one of the core values of the United States is liberty. The right to choose what kind of education an individual aim to yield to his child is a derivative right embodied in the fundamental right to liberty—liberty, which is part of the triple fundamental rights, which are the right to life, the right to liberty, and the right to the pursuit of happiness (property).

When the government involves itself in education to impose uniformity, it intends primarily to undermine the liberty of the learner. It constrains the learner to abide and conform to a set of rules

---

[166] Ibid.

that may not be necessarily beneficial to his full academic potential. Indeed, government intervention into education discourage individuality, innovation, curiosity, creativity an overall excellence. Everybody do not possess the exact same skills and abilities. That is the reason why we, as human beings, are chiefly and elementarily individuals. Even within a family, whereas siblings have the same blood and carry the genes of their parents, they are, nonetheless, principally individuals and therefore, do not possess the same intellectuals abilities and physical skills. By implementing rules based upon general standards to create conformity in a global educational system, the government attempts to impose an unquestionable obedience upon the individual (the learner), and inevitably limits his creativity. In its endeavor to promote equality, government schooling reduces most children to a lowest common customs. I believe education privatization is necessary but not obligatory. Its necessity is established in my belief of the governmental deregulation of the financial monopoly. Government schooling would prevent private actors to improve competitiveness. Private actors should be the primary holders of the financial monopoly that would fund education. In such a free private enterprise exchange economy, government's primary role is to preserve the rules of the game by enforcing contracts, preventing coercion, and keeping markets free[167]. If the government goes beyond its primary role, it then, becomes an encroachment on economic freedom. Privatizing education, beginning with a few districts, would open up the door not to one private competitor but to the whole range of competitors that free markets provide[168]. The success of a private school alternative might lead other entities to conduct their own experiments in communities willing to reduce the effect of public education[169].

---

[167] Article written by Milton, Friedman, and later written by the Editors of EdChoice. "The Role of the Government In Education" *EdChoice,* January 1ˢᵗ, 1962. www.edchoice.org. Article. Web.
[168] Walker, Bruce, "An Argument for Privatizing Public Schools", *New American,* July 27, 2012, www.thenewamerican.com. Article. Web.
[169] Ibid.

Private education enhances innovation and creativity. Private schools and academics that train, for instance, musicians, dancers, and a variety of other young Americans in the rigors of developing natural talent would ensure that the children receive a first class education in the arts as well[170]. So it is quintessential that education becomes more privatized in order to give an equal chance to every children to build their own future.

---

[170] Ibid.

XVI.

On Common Core

The Common Core State Standards Initiative, shortly known as Common Core, is an educational initiative from 2010 that details what K-12 students throughout the United States should know in English language, arts and mathematics at the conclusion of each school grade.[171] The Common Core aim to raise student achievement by standardizing what is taught in schools across the United States, but have sparked controversy among educators, parents, and politicians[172]. For some, the Common Core State Standards seemed to come from nowhere, and appeared to be a sneaky attack on states' rights to control local education[173]. But for those involved in writing the standards, it was nothing short of an exhaustive and collaborative years-long effort aimed at raising the achievement

---

[171] Wikipedia Contributor, "Common Core State Standards", *Wikipedia, the Free Encyclopedia*, September 22, 2018. Web.
[172] Bidwell, Alli, "The History of Common Core State Standards", *US News*, February 27, 2014, www.usnews/news/special-reports/articles/2014/02/27/the-history-of-common-core-state-standards.
[173] Ibid.

160

levels of student across the country[174]. Before politicizing the debate, it is important to understand its history.

Initially, Common Core was created at the state level by the National Governors Association (NGA) and the Council of Chief State School Officers (CCSSO) in 2009 and implemented in 2010. In 2007, the CCSSO gathers state education chiefs at its Annual Policy Forum to begin discussing the need for the standardized test to be implemented at the state level[175]. Education leaders became concerned about the potential for nationwide educational disparities and skewed data on national educational performance[176]. In 2008, though, the two organizations (NGA & CCSSO) believed that Common Core deemed to be a national standardized initiative. In order to nationalized Common Core, the NGA and CCSSO, by the end of 2009, received commitments from the governors of

---

[174] Ibid.

[175] Editors, "Common Core History and Timeline", *HotChalk Education Network*, April 3, 2014. www.hotchalkeducationnetwork.com. Article. Web.

[176] Ibid.

48 states, two territories and Washington, D.C.; to begin creating the Common Core standards[177]. In 2010, the NGA and CCSSO released a revision and invited a feedback from educators and the public—by the end of the year, 39 states join the initiative[178]. The following year, States enacted processes for reviewing ratifying and adopting the Common Core standards[179]. Many states hold public forums to solicit more feedback and continue to leverage work groups assigned to create supplements to the standards for implementation[180].

During the 2016 presidential elections, the debate upon Common Core became a national issue in the context of educational policy. On a personal stance, I am not necessarily a proponent of Common Core although I do understand its intent. Proponents of Common Core States Standards strongly affirm that the initiative provides a national continuity in education. To many

------

[177] Ibid.
[178] Ibid.
[179] Ibid.
[180] Ibid.

educators, the goals of Common Core are eminently reasonable, particularly in states that rank below average or far below average in all-important areas of math and science education[181]. Moreover, proponents of Common Core support uniform standards and conformity. The conformity uplifted by Common Core principles was designed to raise expectations on three core areas, and this conformity recommends a wide list of materials that state and local leaders can choose from to satisfy the standards, but participating in Common Core does not require that those exact texts be taught[182].

My opposition to Common Core is not staunch nor vehement to the point that it must be repealed. Notwithstanding, I believe that its implementation is an encroachment on states' rights' sovereignty. I do believe that a general standard and conformity shall not be incorporated in the educational system at the state level. Curriculums, in my modest opinion, should be left

---

[181] Riley, Robert, "Why I support Common Core" *National Review*. March 25, 2014., www.nationalreview.com. Article. Web.
[182] Ibid.

to local governments of the state, which represent a sovereign entity. As I have reiterated in the previous essay regarding the privatization of education in America, it is surely not the role of the central government to conduct or administer a general, broader, and national curriculum for the sake of elevating the level of success of the learners. I am a firm believer in the principle of local and state's autonomy. It is up to the local governments to take adequate measures to advance a comprehensive curriculum that would facilitate the learning process of the students. Adjunctively, Common Core is based upon an egalitarian philosophy. A philosophy whereby individuals are compelled to be subjected to conformity under the mask of equality—and the entity wearing that mask is nothing else but the government. The philosophy of Common Core utilizes a materialistic approach to enhance its rule of conformity. This materialistic approach is entrenched in standardized test and uniformed curriculum imposed upon diversity.

As a third statement, I believe that one enormous issue with Common Core is that the curriculum does not centrally focus on teaching the student to learn but only to prepare him for the test. When a student is solely taught for the sake of taking the test, it impedes the student's veracity for learning. It only stimulates the student to solitarily concentrate on grades rather than the content of the subject. I personally do not believe that assigning a set of examinations is compulsorily the chief factor to determine the likelihood of success of the students. A student may be a good test-taker, but it does not entail, in any way, that he or she will inevitably succeed at the end. I will use the example of the LSAT to make my point, whereas it is not part of Common Core. The Law School Admission Test (LSAT) is not an objective examination, and having a good score at the test does not grant success in law school and it does not guarantee that one will triumphantly pass the Bar Examination. The student only studies to obtain a good or satisfactory score in order to gain admission to law school. However, having a 165 or 170 on the LSAT does not ultimately ensure that the student will acquire an excellent GPA and successfully pass the Bar. The student mainly focuses on the test and does not learn anything regarding the substance of the subject. It is in that respect that Common Core is established, and subsequently does not prognosticate the success of the learner.

As public education, Common Core enfeebles diversity. Indeed, prescribing the same standards to all states ignores the fact that some students learn different subjects at different paces[183]. Furthermore, States opt into the standards and there is no law that makes Common Core a national curriculum. However, the federal government through the United States Department of Education can, and has used grant competitions like *Race To The Top* to encourage states to adopt school reforms, including Common Core Standards[184]. Government administrative agencies such as *Race To The Top,* give a considerable and significant weight to the federal government's authority to make decisions that would outweigh states' sovereignty on

---

[183] Highman, Michael, "5 Arguments Against Common Core Standards" *IVN*, June 13, 2013, www.ivn.us. Article. Web.
[184] Ibid.

educational matters. Whereas Common Core may reflect some positive aspects, I, however, believe that education in America is not and shall not be nationalized, but strictly be left to state and local governments. State and local governments are closer to the people to understand the needs of the community.

To my personal political understanding, the central government is a gigantic institutional organism that is not closed enough to local communities to comprehend and address their concerns. How can the central government, for instance, design a national curriculum for K-12 students living in Oklahoma or Nevada, with whom it has no direct connections or links? The central government does not know nor perceive the immediate demands that these K-12 Students living in Oklahoma or Nevada, for example, need in order to fulfill the educational prerequisites. Local educational systems, in my opinion, are more equipped to adequately implement a comprehensive curriculum that would keenly contribute to the learner's success.

XVII.

On School Prayers

Schools prayers are mandatory prayers imposed in public schools. In the United States of America, school prayers are prohibited on the legal basis of the First Amendment, which protects religious freedom. The landmark United states Supreme Court case *Engel v. Vitale (1962)* was the adjudicative factor of the interdiction of prayers in public schools. In *Engel v. Vitale (1962)*, the United States Supreme Court ruled that school-sponsored prayer violates the Establishment Clause, which is a provision upon religious liberties. In a 6-1 ruling, the majority stated that the provision allowing students to absent themselves from this activity did not make the law constitutional because the purpose of the First Amendment was to prevent government interference with religion[185]. The court emphasized upon the fact that the government cannot impose a particular religion on any particular system because America is a country wherein the diversity of religious beliefs is also protected by the

---

[185] Editors, "Facts and Case Summary—*Engel v. Vitale (1962)*" *United States Courts.* www.uscourts.gov.

170

Establishment Clause. Since 1962, *Engel v. Vitale* has become the precedential authority upon the injunction of school prayers in America.

The American Religious Right has repudiated this decision upon the legal ground that the United States Supreme Court has miscomprehended the Establishment Clause. It [the Religious Right] argued that in banning school prayer, the United States Supreme Court has mistaken the principle of "Freedom of Religion", guaranteed by the United States Constitution, for freedom *from* religion and any observance of it[186]. Proponents of school prayers believe that school prayers are essential for the development of the student's moral character. Indeed, school prayer advocates argue that school prayers nurture the souls of the students and reinforce the values taught at home and in the community[187]. Moreover, proponents of school prayers hold the belief that the United States is a Judeo-Christian nation. As Christianity being the

---

[186] Editors, "Arguments For Prayer In School" *All About History,* www.allabouthistory.org.
[187] Ibid.

main religion, it is natural that young students are taught from a young age that God exists, that he is real, and it is important that they obey his commandments.

I impetuously oppose prayers in public education, and subsequently stand with the United States Supreme Court's decision to prohibit prayers in public schools. I do stand by my belief for two main reasons. The first reason is grounded in my belief in secularism. Although the United States is predominantly a Judeo-Christian nation, Christianity has never been declared as the official religion of the United States. The United States government has never enacted a law that would institute Christianity as the principal and authoritative religion of the United States. Contrastingly, the United States Constitution has deliberately enforced, since its enactment in 1789, the doctrines of religious liberties for every individuals. It signifies that the United States government is constitutionally powerless to impose a particular religious belief upon individuals. I do, undoubtedly, believe that school prayers violate the principle of the separation of Church and State. Yet, this phrase [Separation of Church and State] is not found in the United States Constitution, it is an accepted principle American law providing that the government cannot interfere in the practices of the Church nor advance or advocate religious observances in government settings[188].

My second argument for standing against school prayers is rooted in the coercive nature of religion. Unquestionably, imposing a religious doctrine upon a student body certainly reflects a coercive method of indoctrinating the student into religious practices that he or she may not be familiar with. Children at a very young age, do not voluntarily pray. I assert this claim because the child at a young age does not fathom the substance of religion. In the private realm, children pray because their parents assign them to do so. It is probably not a problem in the private domain because the choice to endorse a particular religious belief and practice is solemnly entrenched within individual rights.

---

[188] Editors, "Arguments Against Prayer In School" *All About History,* www.allabouthistory.org.

Though, when we swing from the private to the public sphere, the imposition of religious doctrines and practices from a public entity upon an individual, espouses a coercive and dictatorial nature to embrace religion. I am convinced that, when a public entity imposes or commands upon an individual a certain religious practice, it becomes an encroachment and an infringement upon individual liberties. The preservation of individual liberties in the public realm must be and should be absolute. The government is not entitled to enforce religious beliefs and practices upon individuals in public school or any other public entity.

Will *Engel v. Vitale* be one day overturned in the United States Supreme Court? Unlike *Roe v. Wade,* I highly doubt it because the American people have abided to *Engel v. Vitale* as judicial precedent, and it became consequently the law of the land regarding school prayers. School prayers have never been a beneficial element in education in my opinion. Religious beliefs should be contained only and solely in the private sphere, and not beyond the scope of the private realm. At the end of the day, it is because the United States is not theocracy that no religion was declared as the official religion of American civil society. It is because the United States is not a theocracy that the First Amendment via the Establishment Clause protects and guarantees that any individual is free to practice the religion of his or her choice as long as it does not infringe the liberty of others. As the United States is a secular nation, public education shall continue to be so.

XVIII.

On Educational Vouchers

What is school vouchers? From the get-go, school vouchers give parents the freedom to choose a private school for their children, using all or part of the public funding set aside for their children's education[189]. Under such a program, funds typically spent by a school district would be allocated to a participating family in the form of voucher to pay partial or full-tuition for their child's private school[190]. Inevitably, school vouchers represent an essential element in education policy for the American public opinion. Generally, school vouchers is positively perceive by the majority of the American people. But it provokes controversies among educators.

Detractors of school vouchers argue that the program has a negative effect on the educational system. This detrimental effect is based upon three premises. The first premise the educational case. Indeed, opponents of school vouchers argue that

---

[189] Editors, "What is School Vouchers?" *EdChoice.* www.edchoice.org.
[190] Ibid.

178

school vouchers do not improve student's academic performances. According to multiple studies, of the District of Columbia, Milwaukee, and Cleveland schools voucher programs, the targeted population does not perform better in reading and mathematics than students in public schools[191]. Studies further demonstrated that over a period of four years, there was no statistically significant difference between students who were offered a voucher and those who were in their aspirations for future schooling[192]. On the social grounds, opponents of school vouchers maintain that a voucher lottery is a terrible way to determine access to an education[193]. True equity means the ability for every child to attend a good school in the neighborhood[194]. Finally, on the legal premise, about 85 percent of private schools are religious. It signifies that vouchers tend to be a

---

[191] Editors, "10 Reasons Why Private School Vouchers Should Be Rejected". *Americans United For Separation of Church and State.* February 2011. www.au.org. Article. Web.
[192] Ibid.
[193] Editors, "The Case Against School Vouchers". *National Education Association.* www.nea.org.
[194] Ibid.

mean of circumventing the constitutional prohibitions against subsidizing religious practice and instruction[195].

On the matter, I do stand in favor of school vouchers program like the majority of Americans. I believe that school vouchers enhance the freedom of choice. It allows parents to freely choose their child's education. It is a derivative right from the right to liberty. Parents pay taxes for education and should be able to use those tax dollars to educate their children at whichever school they want[196]. A part from the right to choose, school vouchers authorize lower-income students the right to a better education. Whereas I am in favor of private education, public education is still and will always be part of our society.

The right to an education is a fundamental need to promote a better society. Education is the bedrock of the taxpayer—it trains the taxpayer to participate into the economic growth. That is why school

---

[195] Ibid.

[196] Editors, "School Vouchers-Top 4 Pros and Cons" *ProCon.org.* June 8, 2017. www.procon.org. Article. Web.

vouchers are necessary. It provides an access and an opportunity to those living in economic hardship. School vouchers promulgate the kind of equality we, as a society, truly need—the equality that provides us the opportunity to create a life, and a career for ourselves. I do strongly believe in equality of opportunity but not in equality of results. I definitely do not believe in equality of results. I do not believe in equality of outcomes because it subverts the creativity and potential of each individual. School vouchers are the every element of enhancing economic growth through permitting every child to have a contingency to pursue an education. In fact, educating a child in a voucher program usually costs less. Since 2002, the Heritage Foundation reported that the state of Florida, for instance, has been providing $3,500 scholarships to students who qualify as being disadvantages through a tax credit program[197]. This program cost the state about $12 million, but it saved local public

---

[197] Lombardo, Crystal, "14 Pros and Cons of School Vouchers". *Vittana Personal Finance Blog.* www.vittana.org. Article. Web.

school districts $53 million in costs[198]. It implies that the costs of implementing such program worth the costs it requires. School vouchers programs have been a pillar of the educational system in the United States. Its revocation is absolutely not necessary. Instead, school vouchers shall be maintained in order to give a chance to every family in America to live the dream.

---

[198] Ibid.

XIX.

On Vocational Education

Vocational school is a post-secondary program that teaches the necessary skills to help students obtaining work in a specific industry[199]. Interestingly, vocational schools are government-fund programs that, in my opinion, do not acquire enough attention to be discussed, and I, consequently, believe that the issue of vocational school has been undermined by society as a whole, and I think that bestowing a significant consideration to the technical education will solve a lot of issues in the social and economic aspects.

Many people have undermined vocational education because they assert that its essence is not a long-term goal but a short-termed one. Students who complete the programs have a better short-term employment outcomes but struggles to pivot as industries evolve[200]. Other arguments include that, those who are pursuing a vocational education

---

[199] Wikipedia Contributors, "Vocational Education In The United States", *Wikipedia, The Free Encyclopedia.* October 2018. Web.
[200] Barnum, Matt, "The Downside To Career and Technical Education". *The Atlantic.* June 6, 2017, www.theatlantic.com. Article. Web.

are, in fact, not intelligent enough, or do not have the intellectual abilities to sustain in a post-secondary academic education realm. I will use the example of education in the State of Minnesota to demonstrate how vocational education has been subverted and still is. Pro-work Minnesotans are against vocational education because it is to the Minnesotans, a cultural impediment that stands in the way of efforts to enlarge the state's skilled workforce[201]. There is a cultural bias in favor of four-year degrees that pressures many young people into thinking that four years of college is the only valuable route for a student to embrace[202]. The issue on vocational school that evolves in Minnesota is not unique to the State Minnesota, it is throughout the United States. I do personally stands for vocational education and I urge local and state

---

[201] Strurdevant, Lori, " The Bias Against Vocational Education And Technical Training". *StarTribune.* February 2015, www.startribune.com. Article. Web.
[202] Thorman, Catrin, " Lifting the Stigma on Vocational Education and Technical Training". *Center of The American Experiment.* July 5, 2017. www.americanexperiemnt.org. Article. Web.

governments to invest a portion of their budget into the promulgation apprenticeship.

The truth is, vocational education is more beneficial than detrimental, in my opinion. Juvenile prisons are bursting because young folks who are without purpose, without parental guidance, and without formal education, are the perfect scapegoat for the police and for the increase of prison population. With vocational education, these young folks have a chance to escape the ruthlessness of the criminal justice system, also and have an opportunity to shape their life, to give a sense and purpose to their lives. Whereas I disagree with Donald Trump on mostly every issue, I must admit that I agree with him upon his idea and attempt to restore apprenticeship programs within high schools and post-secondary education. Although I am principally opposed to federal government intervention onto social programs, I must acknowledge that if the federal government is inclined to fund apprenticeship programs, it will be adamantly helpful to the millions of people who cannot afford a conventional four-year post-secondary education.

As I have stated, general studies are not for everyone, and that is why vocational education plays a supplementary role in student's career. Not everyone is good at mathematics, biology, history, and other traditional subjects that are characterize college-level work. Not everyone is fascinated by Greek mythology, or by classical music, and overall, not everyone goes to college[203]. Here is why vocational education help these students to orient themselves within a more practical approach and prepares these students for the workforce. The American economy has considerably changed since the last economic crisis of 2008. The manufacturing sector is growing and modernizing, creating a wealth of challenging, well-paying, highly-skilled jobs for those with the skills to do them[204]. The demise of vocational education at the high school level has bred a skills shortage in manufacturing

---

[203] Wyman, Nicholas, "Why We Desperately Need To Bring Back Vocational Training In Schools" *Forbes.* September 1st, 2015. www.forbes.com. Article. Web.
[204] Ibid.

today, and with it a wealth of career opportunities for both under-employed college graduates and high school students and high school students looking for direct pathways to interesting, and lucrative careers[205]. Many of the jobs in manufacturing are attainable through apprenticeships, on-the-job training, and vocational programs offered at community colleges. These institutions do not require expensive, four-years degrees for which many students are not suited[206]. I am convinced that vocational school is one of the greatest alternatives to ensure a job in the workforce for those individuals without a college degree. It, incrementally, ensures the freedom of choice and establishes a more egalitarian concept of opportunity for everyone.

[205] Ibid.
[206] Ibid.

XX.

An Essay On Secularism

This essay was initially not included into this book, but I decided to do it otherwise in order to clarify my position on the matter. The purpose of this essay is not to despise religion at all. It is not to hold religious beliefs in contempt. I am writing this essay to pinpoint a subject that has been at the heart of many debates in American politics and precisely on social issues. The topic is clearly about secularism. Is the United States a secular country? Why secularism is quintessential in American politics? Should the church or religion be the basis to dictate civil policy?

To my understanding, religion itself is a great entity for human condition. We need religion in our lives because the very purpose of religion is to reframe human nature to ethics and morality. Human nature exalts the need to believe in something higher than its own being, a supreme being that has the power to create and destroy, that supreme being that is the master of all things, the master of creation, the creator of living organism, the generator of the being. It is from that conception that the idea of the existence of God was constructed. The human condition finds it essential to abide to the rules of a divine order through the scripts of the holy book in order to live a life of righteousness. So long as the relationship between the human condition and the divine spirit is constrained solely in the private sphere, it is, therefore, not a matter to society. It becomes a matter when the human condition wants to use the divine order upon civil policy.

The United States of America is secular country, whether people do not like to admit it. The United States is a secular nation because the Constitution of the United States, which is the supreme law of the land, has established so under the First Amendment via the Establishment Clause. In my essay entitled *On School Prayers,* I have vehemently epitomized my stance against school prayers because I find it inconceivable that the government subjugates individuals to embrace one specific religion over other religions. The very purpose of the Establishment Clause is to avoid imposing one religious faith over people at the expenses of other religious beliefs.

The separation of religion and government shall always be accentuated because religion is a subject matter upon which human beings will never find a just middle or a common ground. That is one of the main reasons that religious matter shall be left to the private realm. The truth based upon religion is limpidly not objective. Wherefore, any government imposing a vision of truth on its subjects will surely forfeit its legitimacy, and a government which does not sustain the loyalty of its subjects is worthless[207]. A wise government will choose instead to focus on the maintenance of social peace through general rules of conduct that temper passions, moderate behavior, and buffer individuals from inevitable collisions as they pursue their own ends and enterprises, including religious

---

[207] Michael Hayes "James Madison on Religion and Politics: Conservative, Anti-Rationalist, Libertarian" *James Madison And The Future Of Limited Government.* Edited by John Samples. Published by Cato Institute in 2002. ISBN: 9781930865235. P. 156. Print.

194

worship and evangelism[208]. As a matter of fact, the wall of separation between church and state comes into play, however, when Christians move beyond defending group interests and advocate general public policies. It is hard, indeed, to see why nonreligious Americans should find religious arguments for policy positions compelling when Christians disagree over doctrine and dispute the authenticity of one another's faith[209]. When religion is used for political purposes, it empties religion of its eternal meaning and becomes just one more cynical method of acquiring power[210].

The separation of church and state is a constitutional provision that, I believe, must be upheld because it clearly protects every American from passionate discordance and evidently safeguards the liberty of every individual to freely exercise his or her religious belief in the private realm. When religion become the bedrock of civil

---

[208] Ibid. P. 156.
[209] Ibid. P. 159.
[210] James Lankford, Russell Moore, " The Real Meaning of the Separation of Church and State", *Time.* January 16, 2018. www.time.com. Article. Web.

policy, it automatically creates a coercive social order. We must remember that, unlike Saudi Arabia, the United States is not a theocracy and will never be one.

References

1. Wikipedia Contributors, " Popular Sovereignty". Wikipedia, The Free Encyclopedia, August 6, 2018. Web.

2. Patrick, John, "Popular Sovereignty", *Understanding Democracy*, Annenberg Classroom. www.annenbergclassroom.org. Article. Web.

3. Khan, Aliya, "Popular Sovereignty", *Learning To Give,* www.learningtogive.org. Article. Web.

4. Ibid.

5. Ibid.

6. Morris, Christopher W. "The Very Idea of Popular Sovereignty: We The People Reconsidered", *Department of Philosophy, Bowling Green State University* (2000). Article.

7. Ibid.

8. Amar, Akhil Reed, "Of Sovereignty and Federalism". *Yale Law School legal Scholarship Repository.* (1987). Article. Paper 1021.

9. Ibid.

10. "The Declaration of Independence and Natural Rights", *Constitutional Rights Foundation.* www.crf-usa.org. Article. Web.

11. Ibid.

12. Ibid.

13. Ibid.

14. Ibid.

15. "natural rights" *The Columbia Electronic Encyclopedia* (1994).

16. Ibid.

17. Anderson, Owen, "Why the First Amendment is 'First in importance'", *The Washington Times,* (2016). www.washingtontimes.com. Article. Web.

18. Ibid.

19. Ibid.

20. Ibid.

21. Reisner, Avram Israel, "The First Amendment Protects Religious Freedom, But Also Freedom From Religion". *The Baltimore Sun.* (2012). www.articles.baltimoresun.com. Article. Web.

22. Editorial Board, "Our Bedrock, the First Amendment" *Democrat & Chronicle* (2016). www.democratandchronicle.com. Article. Web.

23. Ibid.

24. Wood, Gordon S., "The Third Amendment" *Common Interpretation.* www.constitutioncenter.org. Article, Web.

25. Ibid.

26. Leming, Robert S. "Teaching about the Fourth Amendment's Protection against Unreasonable Searches and Seizures". *ERIC Clearinghouse for Social Studies.* (1993). Article.

27. Ibid.

28. Barnett, Randy E. " The Ninth Amendment: It Means What It Says" *Faculty Scholarship Georgetown University Law Center.* (2006). Article.

29. Ibid.

30. Ibid.

31. Ibid.

32. Utley Jr., Robert L., The Tocqueville Forum, "The Idea of Affirmative Government in American History", *The Promise of American Politics: Principles and Practices After Two Hundred Years.* University Press of America, Inc. (1989). P.17. Print.

33. Ibid. P.17.

34. Ibid. P.17.

35. Ibid. P.18.

36. Palmer, Tom G., "2. Limited Government and the Rule of Law" *Cato Handbook For Policymakers, 8th Edition.* (2017) www.cato.org. Article.37.

37. Shmoop Editorial Team., "Limited Government", Shmoop University Inc. November 11, 2008, www.shmoop.com/constitution/limited-government.

38. Ibid.

39. Penna, Sue Ann, "The Benefits of a Limited Government", *Bloomfield Patch.* (2012). www.patch.com . Article, Web.

40. Ibid.

41. Ibid.

42. Ibid.

43. Ibid.

44. "State's Right" www.u-s-history.com

45. "States' Rights" www.constitution.laws.com

46. Ibid.

47. Ibid.

48. Lawson, Gary, Schapiro, Robert; "The Tenth Amendment" *Common Interpretation.* www.constitutioncenter.org. Article. Web.

49. Ibid.

50. Ibid.

51. Ibid.

52. "Understanding the 10th Amendment". www.constitution.laws.com

53. Cooper, Charles "The Constitution in One Sentence: Understanding the Tenth Amendment". *The Heritage Foundation.* January 10, 2011, www.heritage.org. Article. Web.

54. "What is the Electoral College?" *National Archives and Records Administration.* www.archives.org Article. Web.

55. "Electoral Vote vs. Popular Vote" www.diffen.com Article, Web.

56. Ibid.

57. Ibid.

58. Ibid.

59. Ibid.

60. Ibid.

61. Ibid.

62. "Electoral College" www.history.com. Article. Web.

63. Ibid.

64. Ibid.

65. Ibid.

66. Ibid.

67. England, Trent, "The Electoral College Serves The Interests of All People". *US News,* Nov. 2012. www.usnews.com Article. Web.

68. Wikipedia Contributors. "Isolationism" Wikipedia, The Free Encyclopedia, August 19, 2018. Web.

69. "Isolationism" U.S. History. www.u-s-history.com. Article

70. Ibid.

71. "American Isolationism in the 1930s". *Office of the Historian,* www.history.state.gov. Article.

72. Ibid.

73. Ibid.

74. Ibid.

75. Hunter, Jack, "What's a Neoconservative?" *The American Conservative.* June 23, 2011, www.theamericanconservative.com. Article. Web.

76. Vaisse, Justin, "Neoconservatism and American Foreign Policy". *Brookings.* August 2010, www.brookings.edu. Article. Web.

77. Ehrman, John, "Neoconservatism" *First Principles.* November 2011, www.firstprinciplesjournal.com Article. Web.

78. Ibid.

79. Salam, Reiham, "The United States Doesn't Spend Enough on Its Military". *Slate.* November 2015. www.slate.com. Article.

80. Ibid.

81. Ibid.

82. French, David, "Yes, It is Time to Increase Defense Spending". *National Review*, February 27, 2017. www.nationalreview.com. Article. Web.

83. Ibid.

84. Ibid.

85. Michael Garson, Raj Shah, "America First Shouldn't Mean Cutting Foreign Aid." *The Washington Post.* February 24, 2017. www.washingtonpost.com. Article. Web.

86. Ibid.

87. Ibid.

88. Cumbo, Peter, "Foreign Aid: Good For America, Good For The World", *Public Policy Initiative.* Wharton, University of Pennsylvania. July 9, 2017. www.publipolicy.wharton.upenn.edu. Article.

89. Ibid.

90. Ibid.

91. Ibid.

92. Tremblay-Boire, "US Foreign Aid Explained" *The Conversation.* www.theconversation.com. Article. Web.

93. Ibid.

94. Ibid.

95. Ibid.

96. North Atlantic Treaty Organization (NATO). 1949", *Office of The Historian.* www.history.state.gov. Article.

97. Ibid.

98. Ibid.

99. Ibid.

100. Bonenberger, Adrian, "Against NATO: The Other Side of The Argument". *The Wrath-*

Bearing Tree. October 2016, www.wrath-bearingtree.com. Article. Web.

101.   Ibid.

102.   Ibid.

103.   Ibid.

104.   Ibid.

105.   Ibid.

106.   Ibid.

107.   West, Graham, "The Benefits NATO" *Cagle.* July 12, 2018. www.cagle.com. Article. Web.

108.   Ibid.

109.   Ibid.

110.   Ibid.

111.   Ibid.

112.   Vanden Heuvel, Katrina, "More Than Ever, We Need The UN" *The Nation.* February 20, 2013. www.thenation.com. Article.

113.   "Importance of Funding The UN" *US-UN Partnership.* www.betterworldcamapign.org. Article.

114.   Multilateralism is a political doctrine in international politics that stipulates the implementation of a particular policy through the

consent and mutual agreement of several sovereign nations. Multilateralism is opposed to unilateralism.

115.   Wikipedia Contributors, "Deferred Action for Childhood Arrivals" Wikipedia, the Free Encyclopedia, September 8, 2018.

116.   "Deferred Action for Childhood Arrivals (DACA)" Department of Homeland Security, June 23, 2018. Commentary. www.dhs.gov.

117.   "DACA (Deferred Action for Childhood Arrivals)"*Immigration Equality.* 2015. www.immigrationequality.org. Commentary.

118.   Ibid.

119.   Ibid.

120.   Ibid.

121.   Kopan, Tal, "What Is DACA And Why Is It Ending?" *CNN Politics*, January 2, 2018, www.cnn.com. Article. Web.

122.   Lanktoree, Graham, "Trump Administration Calls On Supreme Court To End DACA". *Newsweek*, January 19, 2018. www.newsweek.com. Article. Web

123.   Rhodan Maya, "When Does DACA Expire? The Supreme Court Just Gave Dreamers More Time", *Time,* February 26, 2018, www.time.com. Article. Web.

124.   Fitzgerald, Kiana, "Here's What DACA Is And Why It's So Important". *Complex.* September 2017, www.complex.com. Article. Web.

125.   Alvarez, Priscilla, "The Border Wall Prototypes Are Up-Now What?" *The Atlantic.* Oct. 26, 2017, www.theatlantic.com. Article. Web

126.   Shelbourne, Mallory, "Trump Officials Make Case For Border Wall". *The Hill.* December, 21, 2017. www.thehill.com. Article. Web.

127.   Rainey, James, "Federal Judge Whom Trump Called 'Mexican' Clears Way For Border Wall". *NBC News.* February 27, 2018, www.nbcnews.com. Article. Web.

128.   Bier, David, "Why The Wall Won't Work" *Cato Institute,* May 2017, www.cato.org. Article. Web.

129.   Ibid.

130.   Ibid.

131.   Salay, Mark, "Would Mexican-US. Border Wall Help or Hurt The Economy?" *Marketplace,* May 1st, 2017. www.marketplace.org. Article. Web.

132.   Ibid.

133.   Felbab-Brown, Vanda, "Why the Border Wall's Costs for Outweigh Its Benefits". *Brookings.* January 30, 2017. www.brookings.edu. Article. Web.

134.   Ibid.

135.   Ibid.

136.   Ibid.

137.   Ibid.

138.   "The Immigration Act of 1990" Laws. www.immigration.laws.com. Commentary.

139.   Ibid.

140.   Goronja, Ariel, "Visa Lottery Program Needs Work, but Has American Value" *Media Milwaukee,* Students-Powered News. University of Wisconsin-Milwaukee. November 24, 2017, www.mediamilwaukee.com. Article. Web.

141.   Ibid.

142.   Congressman Robert Goodlatte, "Visa Lottery Program Is Too Much of A Gamble For Our Nation And Needs To End" *The Hill,* November 6, 2017. www.thehill.com. Opinion. Web.

143.   Ibid.

144.   Ron Nixon, Linda, Qin, "What Is ICE and Why Do Critics Want To Abolish it?" The New York Times. July 3, 2018. www.nytimes.com. Article. Web.

145.   Wikipedia Contributor, "US Immigration and Customs Enforcement". *Wikipedia,* The Free Encyclopedia, September 14, 2018. Web.

146.   Ibid.

147.   Steigerwald, Lucy, "The Case for Abolishing ICE". *The Week,* July 6, 2018, www.theweek.com. Article. Web.

148.   Ibid.

149.   Ibid.

150.   Powell, Dominic, "How To Abolish ICE". *Jacobin,* June 29, 2018. www.jacobinmag.com. Article. Web.

151.   Ron Nixon, Linda, Qin, "What Is ICE and Why Do Critics Want To Abolish it?" The New York Times. July 3, 2018. www.nytimes.com. Article. Web.

152.   Ibid.

153.   Ibid.

154.   The Editors, "Don't Abolish ICE". *National Review*, July 6, 2018. www.nationalreview.com. Article. Web.

155.   Boyd, Kevin, "Here's Why Abolishing ICE Is A Terrible, Horrible, No Good, Very Bad Idea". *The Federalist,* July 11, 2018. www.thefederalist.com. Article. Web.

156.   Ibid.

157.   Godfrey, Elaine, "What 'Abolish ICE' Actually Means". *The Atlantic*, July 11, 2018, www.theatlantic.com. Article. Web.

158.   Antoni Verger, Clara Fontdevila, Adrian Zancaja, "The Privatization of Education: A Political Economy of Global Education Reform", *International Perspective On Education Reform*, (Teachers College Press, Columbia University. 2016) Article.

159.   Ibid.

160.   Ibid.

161.   Editorial Projects in Education Research Center (2004, October 4)"Issues A-Z: Privatization of Public Education" *Education Week.* September 19, 2018 from www.edweek.org/ew/issues/privatization-of-public-education/

162.   Ibid.

163.   Hassard, Jack, "Why Education Must Be Public & Not Privatized", *The National Education Policy Center.* November 19, 2012, www.nepc.colorado.edu. Article. Web.

164.   Ibid.

165.   Hansen, Dale, "Privatization of Public Education Is A Failure", *The Huffington Post*, June 6, 2016. www.huffingtonpost.com. Article. Web.

166.   Ibid.

167.   Article written by Milton, Friedman, and later written by the Editors of EdChoice. "The Role of the Government In Education" *EdChoice,* January 1st, 1962. www.edchoice.org. Article. Web.

168.   Walker, Bruce, "An Argument for Privatizing Public Schools", *New American*, July 27, 2012, www.thenewamerican.com. Article. Web.

169.   Ibid.

170.   Ibid.

171.   Wikipedia Contributor, "Common Core State Standards", *Wikipedia, the Free Encyclopedia*, September 22, 2018. Web.

172.   Bidwell, Alli, "The History of Common Core State Standards", *US News*, February 27, 2014, www.usnews/news/special-reports/articles/2014/02/27/the-history-of-common-core-state-standards.

173.   Ibid.

174.   Ibid.

175.   Editors, "Common Core History and Timeline", *HotChalk Education Network*, April 3, 2014.   www.hotchalkeducationnetwork.com. Article. Web.

176.   Ibid.

177.   Ibid.

178.   Ibid.

179.   Ibid.

180.	Ibid.

181.	Riley, Robert, "Why I support Common Core" *National Review.* March 25, 2014., www.nationalreview.com. Article. Web.

182.	Ibid.

183.	Highman, Michael, "5 Arguments Against Common Core Standards" *IVN*, June 13, 2013, www.ivn.us. Article. Web.

184.	Ibid.

185.	Editors, "Facts and Case Summary—*Engel v. Vitale (1962)*" *United States Courts.* www.uscourts.gov.

186.	Editors, "Arguments For Prayer In School" *All About History,* www.allabouthistory.org.

187.	Ibid.

188.	Editors, "Arguments Against Prayer In School" *All About History,* www.allabouthistory.org.

189.	Editors, "What is School Vouchers?" *EdChoice.* www.edchoice.org.

190.	Ibid.

191.	Editors, "10 Reasons Why Private School Vouchers Should Be Rejected". *Americans*

United For Separation of Church and State. February 2011. www.au.org. Article. Web.

192.   Ibid.

193.   Editors, "The Case Against School Vouchers". *National Education Association.* www.nea.org.

194.   Ibid.

195.   Ibid.

196.   Editors, "School Vouchers-Top 4 Pros and Cons" *ProCon.org.* June 8, 2017. www.procon.org. Article. Web.

197.   Lombardo, Crystal, "14 Pros and Cons of School Vouchers". *Vittana Personal Finance Blog.* www.vittana.org. Article. Web.

198.   Ibid.

199.   Wikipedia Contributors, "Vocational Education In The United States", *Wikipedia, The Free Encyclopedia.* October 2018. Web.

200.   Barnum, Matt, "The Downside To Career and Technical Education". *The Atlantic.* June 6, 2017, www.theatlantic.com. Article. Web.

201.   Strurdevant, Lori, " The Bias Against Vocational Education And Technical Training".

StarTribune. February 2015, www.startribune.com. Article. Web.

202. Thorman, Catrin, " Lifting the Stigma on Vocational Education and Technical Training". *Center of The American Experiment.* July 5, 2017. www.americanexperiemnt.org. Article. Web.

203. Wyman, Nicholas, "Why We Desperately Need To Bring Back Vocational Training In Schools" *Forbes.* September 1st, 2015. www.forbes.com. Article. Web.

204. Ibid.

205. Ibid.

206. Ibid.

207. Michael Hayes "James Madison on Religion and Politics: Conservative, Anti-Rationalist, Libertarian" *James Madison And The Future Of Limited Government.* Edited by John Samples. Published by Cato Institute in 2002. ISBN: 9781930865235. P. 156. Print.

208. Ibid. P.156.

209. Ibid. P.159.

210. James Lankford, Russell Moore, " The Real Meaning of the Separation of Church and

State", *Time.* January 16, 2018. www.time.com. Article. Web.